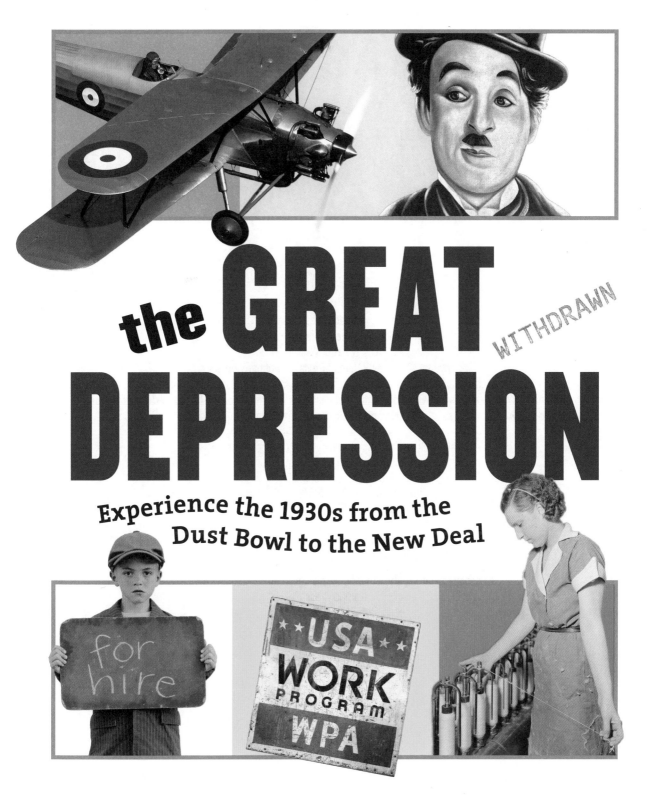

the GREAT DEPRESSION

WITHDRAWN

Experience the 1930s from the Dust Bowl to the New Deal

INQUIRE AND INVESTIGATE

Marcia Amidon Lusted
Illustrated by Tom Casteel

Nomad Press
A division of Nomad Communications
10 9 8 7 6 5 4 3 2 1

This book was manufactured by Marquis Book Printing,
Montmagny, Québec, Canada
February 2016, Job #120818
ISBN Softcover: 978-1-61930-340-9
ISBN Hardcover: 978-1-61930-336-2

Illustrations by Tom Casteel
Educational Consultant, Marla Conn

Questions regarding the ordering of this book should be addressed to
Nomad Press
2456 Christian St.
White River Junction, VT 05001
www.nomadpress.net

Printed in Canada.

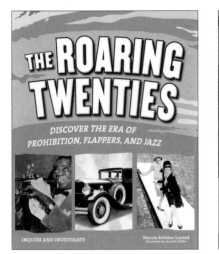

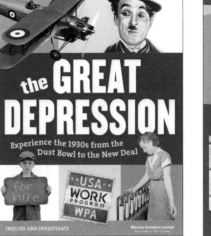

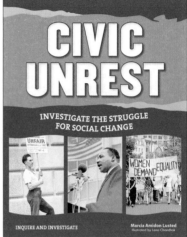

Social studies titles in the
Inquire and Investigate series

Check out more titles at www.nomadpress.net

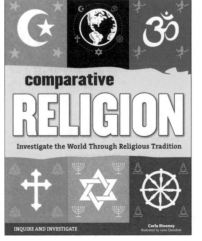

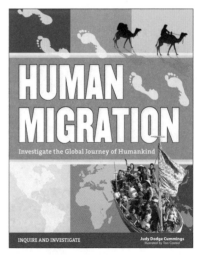

Interested in primary sources?

PS

Look for this icon.

You can use a smartphone or tablet app to scan the QR codes and explore more about the Great Depression! Cover up neighboring QR codes to make sure you're scanning the right one. You can find a list of each URL on the Resources page.

If the QR code doesn't work, try searching the Internet with the Keyword Prompts to find other helpful sources. 🔍

Contents

TIMELINE

1929 .... **October 29:** The stock market crashes on Black Tuesday.

1930 .... The differential analyzer computer is developed at MIT.

February 18: Clyde Tombaugh discovers the planet Pluto.

August 12: Clarence Birdseye successfully creates freeze-dried food.

1931 .... **March 3:** "The Star-Spangled Banner" becomes the official national anthem.

April 11: The Empire State Building is completed.

1932 .... Unemployment reaches 25 percent.

Scientists John Cockcroft and Ernest Walton split the atom.

The Bonus Army marches on Washington, DC.

March 1: The Lindbergh baby is kidnapped.

May 20–21: Amelia Earhart is the first woman to fly solo across the Atlantic.

November 8: Franklin Roosevelt defeats Herbert Hoover in the presidential election.

1933 .... Adolf Hitler is appointed chancellor of Germany.

March 4: Roosevelt is inaugurated and begins launching New Deal programs.

March 9–June 16: The first hundred days of Roosevelt's administration see many new programs created.

March 9: The Emergency Banking Act is passed.

March 31: The Civilian Conservation Corp is authorized.

April 19: The United States is officially off the gold standard.

May 27: The Century of Progress World's Fair begins in Chicago.

December 5: Prohibition ends with the passage of the 21st Amendment.

1934 .... The first dust storms that will come to be known as the Dust Bowl begin.

May 28: The Dionne quintuplets are born in Canada.

June 6: The Securities Exchange Act is signed.

TIMELINE

1935 .... **April14:** Black Sunday, one of the biggest, most frightening dust storms, takes place.

July 17: The first parking meter is installed.

August 14: The Social Security program is enacted.

September 30: The Hoover Dam is dedicated.

1936 .... **June 10:** The book *Gone With the Wind* is published.

November 3: Roosevelt defeats Landon in the presidential election.

1937 .... Japan invades China.

January/February: Massive flooding takes place along the Ohio River.

May 6: The Hindenburg zeppelin explodes in New Jersey.

May 27: The Golden Gate Bridge opens in San Francisco.

June: Amelia Earhart disappears during a flight around the world.

1938 .... The first *Superman* comic book is published.

The first Volkswagen Beetle car is sold in Germany.

January: The first full-length cartoon, *Snow White and the Seven Dwarfs*, debuts.

March: German Chancellor Hitler annexes Austria.

June 25: A federal minimum wage is established.

October 22: Chester Carlson invents the photocopier.

October 30: Orson Welles broadcasts *The War of the Worlds* on the radio, causing a national panic.

1939 .... World War II begins in Europe.

Igor Sikorsky invents the helicopter.

The Wizard of Oz movie premieres.

April 30: The New York World's Fair opens.

1940 .... Bugs Bunny debuts in the cartoon *A Wild Hare*.

Roosevelt becomes the first president ever elected to three terms.

1941 .... M&Ms are created.

December 7: The Japanese attack the naval base at Pearl Harbor, Hawaii.

December 8: The United States enters World War II.

Introduction ▶

A Turbulent Time

Why were the 1930s a difficult decade for many people?

 Many things happened during the 1930s that created hardship for lots of people. These included a huge economic depression, an environmental crisis, and a war brewing in Europe. But there were good things that happened as well.

The 1930s is a decade with many nicknames, such as "The Dirty Thirties," "The Turbulent Thirties," or "The Starving Thirties." When referring to the 1930s, historians often talk about the Great Depression and the Dust Bowl. The decade of the 1930s was a time of great hardship for many. It was also a time of amazing inventions. The 1930s saw the birth of government programs that we still use today, such as Social Security and insured bank deposits. What makes the 1930s so different from all the other decades?

A CRASH STARTS IT ALL

In 1929, America was still embracing the "roaring" twenties, which was a decade of affluence for many people. Life changed dramatically in the 1920s. There was more money to spend and more to spend it on. People found new roles to enjoy and focused more on leisure time and having fun.

It seemed as though many Americans were enjoying a party that would never end, even though some people, such as farmers and minorities, never really shared in the general prosperity of the times. The party did end, though, with the Stock Market Crash of 1929 that ushered in a period of hard times. The economy did not fully recover from the Great Depression until World War II. It affected an entire generation of people.

[An economic depression is an extreme recession that lasts two years or more.]

This is a period of time when personal income, prices, and profits all drop. It is characterized by increased unemployment, less available credit, and reduced trading and commerce. If a depression lasts for too long, consumers lose confidence and stop investing. Did your family or someone you know experience any effects from the most recent recession, which began in 2007? Are you, or they, still feeling those effects?

Later in 1929, Americans suddenly found themselves losing their jobs and having their homes foreclosed on. Many people lost the money in their savings accounts. Between 1930 and 1933, 9,000 banks failed. Imagine going to the bank to withdraw money and finding it closed forever. This happened to many people.

Today, we talk about 8 percent unemployment being unacceptably high, but the early 1930s saw 25 percent unemployment. One quarter of the American work force was unemployed.

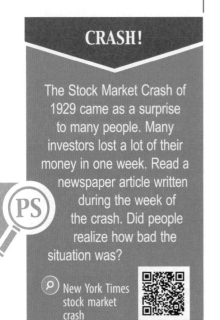
Before 1933, there were no federal government programs in place to help people who lost their jobs. Today, unemployment insurance helps people take care of themselves until they can find another job. Without money to spend, unemployed consumers no longer shopped. Business after business closed, and people whose livelihoods depended on manufacturing or selling goods lost their jobs as well.

It was also a decade of severe natural disasters. The Great Plains states, including Colorado, Texas, Kansas, Oklahoma, and New Mexico, suffered through one of the worst droughts ever recorded.

[The dry conditions spawned huge dust storms, blowing loose topsoil in "black blizzards" of dust and dirt.]

It was impossible to grow crops in these conditions. Millions of farmers and agricultural workers were forced to leave their farms and homes. Many traveled to places such as California in search of work.

Stratford, Texas, 1935

photo credit: National Oceanic and Atmospheric Administration/ Department of Commerce

At first, the government did little that helped. It wasn't until President Franklin Roosevelt was elected in 1932 that the government began to put policies and programs into place that were designed to help the economy. These programs also began to help people who had no way to earn money or feed their families.

SHAPING A GENERATION

The Great Depression shaped an entire generation of Americans. Many of those who grew up during the 1930s always carried with them the memory of hunger and hardship. Many of them were thrifty and distrustful of banks and credit all of their lives.

Because of the Great Depression, the U.S. government changed the way it regulated banking and commerce. Many of the protective programs we still have today were created during this time.

In *The Great Depression*, you'll discover how the struggles of the 1930s shaped the character of American society. You'll learn about this difficult time between the modern world that appeared in the 1920s and the era of the Second World War and the prosperous society it created. What was it like to be an American living during such a turbulent time?

VOCAB LAB

There is a lot of new vocabulary in this book! Turn to the glossary in the back when you come to a word you don't understand. Practice your new vocabulary in the **Vocab Lab** activities in each chapter.

1930s FACTOID

During the 1930s, doctors earned about $61 per week, while factory workers earned about $17 per week. In 2014, the average weekly earnings for factory jobs were $465. For doctors, the average weekly salary was more than $3,000.

KEY QUESTIONS

- Why do we still have economic depressions? Do people learn from history?
- Do you know anyone who lived during the Great Depression? Do they have any habits that might have formed during the 1930s?
- What contemporary events might shape your worldview when you are an adult?

COMPARE THE DECADES

In 2008, a recession took place in the United States that seemed to echo the Great Depression of the 1930s. Called the Great Recession, it was a time when unemployment spiked in 2008 and 2009 and many people lost their homes. How was this recession similar to the Great Depression?

Forbes
depression
compare
recession

- **Read this article comparing the Great Recession of 2008 to the Great Depression of the 1930s.** What is similar? What is different?

- **Create a chart comparing the Great Depression with the 2008 recession.** Look at indicators such as the stock market, unemployment, housing foreclosures, bank failures and bailouts, and government reactions and programs.

- **Do you think the Great Depression could happen again in your lifetime?** Why or why not? Create another chart showing how the current decade is different or similar to the 1930s.

To investigate more, create a Venn diagram to show what was similar about the United States before the Great Depression and the Great Recession. Venn diagrams are made of characteristics written in circles that overlap. In the overlapping section write the things about the country that were similar. In the sections that don't overlap, write the things that were different.

Chapter 1

Boom to Bust

How did the good times of the Roaring Twenties become the hard times of the Great Depression?

 Not everyone enjoyed prosperity during the 1920s, and there were signs throughout that decade that the good times were not going to last.

Can you imagine living in a time when everyone seemed to be making lots of money? There are new inventions, new things to buy, and it seems as though things are only going to get better and better! Many Americans living in the 1920s felt this way. Life was a party and they thought that the party would never end. But when the stock market crashed in October 1929, the party finally came to a screeching halt. At least, it's easy to use that event to mark the end of the Roaring Twenties. However, the warning signs were there for many years before the crash took place.

ROARING AND WHIMPERING

The decade of the 1920s was called the Roaring Twenties for good reason. It was a time when the economy, society, and the conveniences of modern life were all changing and evolving at a rapid pace.

Buying and selling stocks on the stock market became an activity that many people could do. It was a way to become rich without having to work very hard. Stocks are basically small pieces of companies that people own when they purchase that stock. Buying stock became a fad.

Many people didn't know or care whether the investments they were making were good or bad. It didn't even matter if the companies they were buying stock in were solid companies worth the investment.

[This crazy buying frenzy pushed the price of stocks much higher than they should have been.]

Many buyers didn't even have the money to buy stocks. They bought stocks on margin, meaning that they put down a small down payment and borrowed the rest of the money from their broker to purchase those stocks. This kind of investing is incredibly risky because if the value of the stock falls, the debt to the broker is still owed for the full amount of what was borrowed.

There were other signs that things were not as good as people believed. Consumers carried more debt than ever before. They were able to do this because of the ability to buy on credit instead of paying cash for goods. This meant that someone could enjoy more and more consumer goods even if they couldn't afford to buy them outright.

Buying on credit became a problem as wages began to fall. When people who already had debts could not afford to keep buying consumer goods, production at factories fell. This led to unemployment, as factories began to lay off some of their workers. Fewer workers were needed to produce fewer goods.

Another factor leading toward economic downfall was the fact that the amount of wealth in the United States was unevenly and unfairly distributed. A small percentage of wealthy people had most of the money, while most Americans had far less. Farmers, minorities, and people with low-paying jobs barely had any money at all.

Banks had invested their customers' money too heavily in stocks. In addition, the banks had granted many large loans that now people could not afford to repay. That meant there was even less actual money available for these banks to lend. At that time, banks weren't regulated by the government. This means there were no rules in place about how they operated and how they could use their depositors' money. Banks were not insured by the federal government, either.

All of these things built up quietly in the last few years before the stock market crash on October 29, 1929. On that day, stock prices began to fall. This caused people to panic and try to sell their shares while they could still make money from them. This selling made the market fall even faster.

[
On that October day, nicknamed Black Tuesday, 16,410,030 shares of stock were traded at lower and lower prices. Investors lost millions of dollars.
]

Soon, stocks were worth barely a fraction of what they had been valued at when the stock market peaked. In addition, banks that had invested in the stock market lost money that belonged to their customers.

> Many depositors lined up outside their banks to withdraw their deposits in cash, but the banks did not have enough money to go around. Many simply closed.

In just a few short weeks, $30 billion of investment money evaporated. During that time, some wealthy Americans, such as John D. Rockefeller, bought up large amounts of stock, hoping to bolster the market. Some large corporations actually announced that they would give their investors bigger dividends on their stocks, to increase confidence. The stock exchange shortened its hours. But none of these rescue tactics worked.

The Roaring Twenties ended with a whimper. The good times were over and the Great Depression had begun.

WHAT HAPPENED NEXT?

Where did most people first look for help? Naturally, they looked to their government. The country was in trouble and many believed that President Herbert Hoover had to take action.

The first thing President Hoover did was to propose to Congress that the taxes on individuals and corporations should be reduced. He hoped that if Congress agreed, people wouldn't have to pay so much in taxes and this would help the economy.

Hoover also met with some of the biggest industrial groups in the United States. These included bankers, the executives of railroads and other large industries, and labor and farm leaders. He asked them for their assurance that they would keep spending money and not cut workers' wages. Hoover asked governors and mayors all over the country to expand public works projects as a way to create new jobs. He also increased the amount of money that the federal government was willing to spend on new federal building projects.

These actions were taken to reassure people and industries that the economic crash was just temporary. Hoover hoped that things would be back to normal by the next spring.

Did these measures work? On the outside, it seemed to. Newspapers ran ads that said things such as, "All right, Mister—now that the headache is over, LET'S GO TO WORK," and insisted that even with the stock sellout, regular people in towns and cities were still buying goods. In the spirit of this confidence, one of the most popular songs of that time was called "Happy Days Are Here Again."

> Even with efforts to make the economic downturn seem like a temporary thing, most people knew better.

Many people had lost a great deal of money in the stock market crash and they had to start economizing right away. They stopped spending money on anything that wasn't absolutely necessary.

Even wealthy people and businesses cut their spending. Because factories were making fewer goods, they had to postpone building additional facilities. They had to get rid of jobs. Banks, which were still reeling from losses in the stock market, found themselves holding onto foreclosed properties from people who could no longer pay their mortgages. Happy days were definitely not here again.

A MOMENT OF OPTIMISM

There were some small signs of hope. Investors and speculators—people who took chances on investments or stocks that might become valuable again—leaped back into the stock market. They believed that the crash had simply been a downturn, which is not uncommon. They were sure that the worst was over, so they began buying stocks in companies that they believed would recover quickly. This led to a small surge in the stock market as the volume of trading increased.

This moment of optimism was just that, a moment. Even while stock prices seemed to rise, all it took was a good look around to see that the country was still in serious economic trouble. Prosperity was not going to happen again anytime soon.

Most of the rebounding energy went toward businesses that were consolidating, or growing smaller, rather than those that were getting started or expanding.

There was so much that was still wrong with the economy. In the winter of 1932-33, unemployment was the worst that had ever been recorded. In some cities, hundreds or even thousands of men without jobs gathered and marched to call attention to how bad things were for them and their families.

> By April 1930, stock prices were falling again and the index that measured how businesses were doing was also falling.

President Hoover still insisted that everything would be fine again by the fall, saying, "We have now passed the worst and with continued unity of effort we shall rapidly recover." But Americans were no longer so likely to believe his assurances.

TARIFFS, PRICE CONTROLS, AND DROUGHT

Several things happened to show that the economy was still in trouble, despite President Hoover's efforts and assurances. Congress revised America's tariffs, which are the taxes or duties that are paid on any goods that are imported into the country. These tariffs made it more expensive for companies in foreign countries to send their goods to the United States for sale. These foreign countries were not happy about America's tariffs. They retaliated by imposing or increasing their own tariffs on American goods. Now it was even harder for American companies to make money selling their products overseas.

Meanwhile, the Federal Farm Board had been trying to keep the prices of wheat and cotton high, to benefit farmers. The board bought up excess crops to keep prices from falling.

By the end of the 1930 growing season, the Federal Farm Board had accumulated 60 million bushels of wheat and more than 1 million bales of cotton. But all this buying only slowed the fall of prices. It did not halt the fall in prices completely.

Then a terrible drought stretched from the East Coast to the Midwest, causing crops to fail and wells to dry up. Unemployment rose again, leaving a total of almost 6 million people out of work by the end of the year.

Hoover believed that the American people must heal the economy themselves, not rely on the government to do it for them. He believed in "rugged individualism," in Americans pulling themselves back to prosperity through hard work. But the deteriorating economy wasn't something that average Americans could fix just by working hard.

There were other factors slowing down the economy after a long period of economic expansion. Since the end of the nineteenth century, the country had been growing at a rapid pace. The Industrial Revolution had created many new inventions and machines for producing goods more quickly and easily. Natural resources such as coal, oil, and metals had been discovered and exploited by big companies.

HEAL THYSELF

President Hoover said, "Economic depression cannot be cured by legislative action or executive pronouncement. Economic wounds must be healed by the action of the cells of the economic body—the producers and consumers themselves."

In his 1920 autobiography, Andrew Carnegie, a multimillionaire industrialist, explained his views on why American industry will grow through capitalism, both at home and in other countries.

"One great advantage which America will have in competing in the markets of the world is that her manufacturers will have the best home market. Upon this they can depend for a return upon capital, and the surplus product can be exported with advantage, even when the prices received for it do no more than cover actual cost, provided the exports be charged with their proportion of all expenses. The nation that has the best home market, especially if products are standardized, as ours are, can soon outsell the foreign producer."

[Capitalism had evolved as new types of companies and new business practices developed.]

But all this economic development could not continue indefinitely. Natural resources don't last forever. There were fewer new places in the world to explore and to use for economic possibilities. The economy itself was more complicated and couldn't handle large amounts of debt as it might have once.

All of this expansion had made Americans feel that the economy would charge ahead, no matter what. It had given them the false sense that they could add debt, increase credit, and zoom ahead by speculating in stocks and real estate without any problems.

The worst was not over, no matter what President Hoover said. The government might argue about tariffs and manufacturing and expanding industry, but the average American knew that it all came down to whether or not they had a job. Without a job, they could not feed their families or keep their homes or buy what they needed. And as 1930 became 1931, having a job became something Americans could no longer rely on.

KEY QUESTIONS

- Why were the 1920s such an exciting time? Did people make smart choices during this decade? Why or why not?

- What are some of the reasons the stock market crashed in 1929?

- Did President Hoover make smart choices about how to handle the stock market crash?

REPORT THE NEWS

It's October 29, 1929, and the stock market is experiencing Black Tuesday. Investors are panicking and trade 16 million shares and lose billions of dollars in a single day.

- **Imagine that you are a reporter for a major radio network.** Remember, people in the 1920s get their news from newspapers and radio. You are told to report on the panic that's taking place at the New York Stock Exchange.

- **Create a radio broadcast interview in which you give an overview of the situation.** You'll want to speak to many different people about what is happening. Write a script for this broadcast, and then, with the help of your classmates, act it out and record it.

- **Interview a mix of people.** These can include a stockbroker, bank manager, someone who runs a business, people on the street who have invested in stocks and lost everything, even a politician. You can incorporate sound effects from city streets or the stock market trading floor. Why would some people not be worried about what was happening?

> To investigate more, find an audio recording or a video clip from a newsreel of an actual report or interview from Black Tuesday. What was the overall tone of the report? How did people react? Were there any attempts by that media source to calm the fears of the public? Try searching these key words: video Black Tuesday 1929.

VOCAB LAB 📖

Write down what you think each word means:

insured, **dividends**, **optimism**, **tariffs**, **individualism**, and **exploit**.

Compare your definitions with those of your friends or classmates. Did you all come up with the same meanings? Turn to the text and glossary if you need help.

Inquire & Investigate

1930s SLANG

The 1920s was the first decade to emphasize youth culture over the older generations. Young people often use slang to create new words that become mainstream with time. Some 1930s slang words are still used today!

Aces, snazzy, swell: very good

All wet: no good

Peepers, shutters, blinkers: eyes

INVEST!

When you buy a share of stock in a company, you are actually buying a piece of the company and becoming a shareholder. Each share, or piece, of the company costs money. When the company makes money, so do the shareholders.

What is it like to invest in the stock market, as so many people did in the 1920s?

- **Think about some of the familiar brands you see every day.** Some of these might be companies such as PepsiCo (PEP), Google (GOOG), Nike (NKE) or Apple (AAPL). These are all well-known companies that are publicly traded. Choose one company that you are going to "buy" stock in.

- **Go to nasdaq.com.** Enter the symbol for the stock or enter the company's name to get the symbol. Look at the cost (value) of one share of stock. Click on the "intraday" graph, which shows the daily activity of the stock and how the value can quickly change. Click on the 5 day, 1 month, 6 months, and 1 year charts and read the graphs. Note the changes in the stock's price across the different time periods.

- **Decide how much stock you would like to buy.** For example, if you buy 1,000 shares of PepsiCo for $68.00 per share, you can calculate the value of your shares by multiplying:

$68.00 x 1,000 shares = $68,000.00 total value

- **Make a chart like the one below and follow the stock for a week.** At the end of each day, check your stock, fill in the stock price, and multiply the price by 1,000 to find the total value of your shares each day.

Day:	Stock Price:	Total Value of 1,000 Shares:
Monday		
Tuesday		
Wednesday		
Thursday		
Friday		

- **On Friday, do a final assessment of your stock's value.** Think about what you learned from the activity. What do you think you should do with your stock—sell, hold, or buy more? Are you ready to become a "shareholder" in another company?

To investigate more, look at the week's news. Were there any national or global news stories, dramatic weather, or political events that could have affected the price of your stock in the company you chose? Try buying five different stocks and track their progress for a month. Is it better to buy stocks that are all in similar companies or is it better to have a mix of stocks from a variety of companies?

Chapter 2 ▶
Not a Job in Sight

Why did so many people lose their jobs because of the Great Depression?

Employment is directly linked to the health of the economy. As soon as the stock market crashed, it set up a chain of events that led to massive joblessness.

In January 1929, more than 30,000 men lined up in the frigid winter weather at the Ford Motor Company's huge River Rouge factory near Dearborn, Michigan. About 40,000 employees already worked there, but the Ford Motor Company had advertised that it needed to hire 30,000 more workers. Despite the fact that the stock market crash was still several months in the future and times were still thought to be prosperous, the men had come from many different states hoping to get a job. This was a clue that times were not as good as everyone claimed and that bigger problems loomed for the U.S. economy.

Fast-forward a year or two. The stock market has crashed. Regular people who had invested their money in stocks have seen their savings swept away. Many still owed their brokers the money they had borrowed to buy the stocks. Lots of people had to sell their cars and even their homes to pay this debt.

Imagine that you were one of the lucky workers who got one of those coveted jobs at the River Rouge factory back in 1929. Suddenly, you're laid off. You've lost your job because so many other people have lost their savings and jobs. People out of work who are already in debt are no longer buying cars. The demand for new automobiles has fallen drastically in a short period of time.

> Fewer people buying cars means fewer cars need to be made, and that requires fewer workers.

This wasn't just happening in the automobile industry. Many factories and businesses were forced to cut back their labor forces or even close their doors. People who were lucky enough to keep their jobs might find that they had their wages reduced. Or maybe they were working fewer hours, which means they were getting paid for fewer hours. By 1932, the unemployment rate in the United States was 25 percent. That means that one of every four people of working age in the country did not have a job. In 1932, at least 12 million people were out of work.

The country was officially in a depression. There had been depressions in the United States before, and they were actually considered to be a normal part of a growing capitalist economy. Previous depressions had hurt poor people, but most of the time people in the middle and upper classes of income and wealth had been only mildly affected.

GOODBYE, GOODBYE

This poem ran in *The New York Times* on November 3, 1929.

As fall the leaves by Autumn blown,

So fell those lovely shares I own.

Forlorn, disconsolate I sing,

Goodbye, goodbye to everything!

To car and plane and gleaming yacht

And rather ducal country cot

That all seemed surely mine by Spring,

Goodbye, goodbye to everything!

PENNY AUCTIONS

During the 1920s and 1930s, many farmers lost their farms to foreclosure when they could no longer afford to pay their mortgages and loans. Most of these farms and their equipment were sold at public auction. However, farmers banded together to help each other by attending these auctions and bidding ridiculously low amounts for buildings and equipment, such as one penny. With no other bidders, the bank would be forced to accept the bid. Then the farmer who purchased the item would turn around and give it back to the farmer whose farm was being auctioned off.

But this depression, which came to be called the Great Depression, was much worse. It affected more people, both rich and poor. And to make things worse, many people had moved away from farms to the cities when times were good. Now, without jobs, they had no way to grow any food.

Farmers, who could at least feed their families from their land, had suffered from low crop prices for years. Some actually destroyed some products, such as milk and grain, because they could not sell them for a fair price. Some people were starving while others were throwing away extra food.

NO SAFETY NETS

What happens today when someone loses their job? They might receive unemployment insurance or welfare. There are federal programs in place to make sure that people don't go hungry. This is called a safety net.

Before 1933, there weren't any safety nets. Welfare and unemployment insurance did not exist. In fact, President Hebert Hoover did not believe that the government should help individuals. "I do not believe that the power and duty of the general government ought to be extended to the relief of individual suffering," he said in 1930.

Hoover kept a nonintervention policy until 1931. This means that he kept the government from becoming directly involved in providing relief, including money or other forms of help, to the American people. "The lesson should be constantly enforced that though the people support the government, the government should not support the people," he said.

> Unfortunately, he spoke these words at a time when many Americans went to bed hungry. Many didn't even have a place to sleep at night.

In the 1930s, if you lost your job, you instantly lost any kind of money coming in to feed your family and pay your mortgage and cover other costs and debts. If they were lucky enough to have savings, most people used them up just staying alive. After that, they might lose their homes and be forced to either move in with relatives or go on the road, looking for jobs.

By 1932, there were approximately a million people, both single people and in families, roaming the country. They drove ramshackle cars, hitchhiked, or rode trains illegally because they no longer had homes and were seeking any kind of work they could find. When word went out about a company or a project that was hiring workers, people often flocked there in large numbers. It didn't matter if it was halfway across the country.

The Boulder Dam, later renamed the Hoover Dam, 1941

photo credit: Ansel Adams, U.S. National Archives

HOOVER DAM

Watch a video made about the Boulder Dam in 1930. Who do you think the video is meant for? What are the benefits of building the Hoover Dam? What are some of the dangers faced by the workers?

PS

🔍 Hoover Dam video national archives

President Hoover believed that people should help themselves. He felt that if the government helped businesses, then that would strengthen the overall economy and eventually help individual citizens.

PS

1930s FACTOID

In his book *The Grapes of Wrath*, John Steinbeck tells the story of the Joad family, which travels across the country in search of work. He writes, "How can you frighten a man whose hunger is not only in his own cramped stomach but in the wretched bellies of his children? You can't scare him—he has known a fear beyond every other."

In 1931, the government announced a huge new construction project. The Boulder Dam would be constructed on the Colorado River near Las Vegas, Nevada. The project would require about 5,000 workers and would last for years. Workers would be provided with homes in a specially constructed town. News of the need for workers circulated years before actual construction began, and people began streaming to what was then the tiny town of Las Vegas.

Leo Dunbar, who lived in Las Vegas at that time, described these desperate job seekers.

> Not only the men, but their families came with them. They just picked up whatever they had and loaded it into a truck and drove here, and had hopes of getting a job. There had been thousands of people that had moved in here.

Families camped in the central square in Las Vegas as well as all along the dusty roads nearby. Because of the overwhelming numbers of people camping in the surrounding area, President Hoover moved construction of Boulder Dam forward by six months. The dam was later renamed Hoover Dam.

A BONUS ARMY

Another group of people who had lost their jobs and were hungry and homeless were men who had served the country during World War I. In 1924, Congress voted to give veterans a bonus of about $1,000 per man in appreciation for their service. The bonus was due to be paid in 1945. But as the depression grew worse, these veterans demanded that they get the money promised to them right away, when they needed it.

Thousands of veterans marched into Washington, DC, to demand that the president pay the bonuses early.

Some soldiers marched, despite having lost arms and legs or suffered other injuries in the war. Many brought their families along.

Since they didn't have jobs or money, they had to sleep wherever they could. Some camped in empty buildings and others in tents or shacks put up in public areas. As many as 20,000 members of what came to be called the Bonus Army came to Washington in hopes of convincing the government to pay the bonuses early. But the government voted no.

Many members of the Bonus Army stayed in Washington after the government said no to early bonuses. When they still had not left after several weeks, the U.S. Army used tear gas and guns to drive them out of the city. Their shanties and tents were torn down or burned. Many people were injured and several were killed. Hoover showed no remorse. He felt that the army had quelled a threat to the government and public safety. "A challenge to the authority of the United States Government has been met, swiftly and firmly," Hoover said.

THE BONUS ARMY

The Bonus Army was determined to get its bonus, even though it was years before it was scheduled to be paid. Were veterans right in demanding their money? Was Hoover wrong to send the U.S. Army to disperse the crowd? Watch this video of the demonstration. Do the marchers seem peaceful? How can you tell?

 Bonus Army video

HOOVERVILLES

What do you think it would be like to live in a flimsy shack instead of a real house or apartment? You can see pictures of shantytowns and the people who lived there. Do you think these were healthy places to live?

PS

🔍 Hoovervilles video

What did people do when they lost their jobs and homes? Some went out into the street to beg. Sherwood Anderson, a well-known writer of the time, described what he was seeing.

> Men who are heads of families [are] creeping through the streets of American cities, eating from garbage cans; men turned out of houses and sleeping week after week on park benches, on the ground in parks, in the mud under bridges . . . . Our streets are filled with beggars, with men new to the art of begging.

People who lost their homes turned to friends or relatives to take them in. Those who did not have anyone to turn to began creating any kind of shelter that they could. One couple, evicted from their New York City apartment because they could not pay their rent, ended up living in a cave in the city's Central Park.

Other families built shanties out of scraps of wood, old boxes and boards, tarpaper, and discarded metal. Anything that might make some sort of protection from the weather was used to create a shelter. These people usually had open campfires outside to warm themselves and cook over.

Shantytowns such as this sprang up all over the country. They came to be called Hoovervilles, named after President Hoover. Even though Hoover claimed to be doing what he could to help Americans suffering from the Great Depression, he had not been effective. Many blamed him for the worsening crisis.

Food was also scarce. Some people begged for food on the street. As the Great Depression deepened, many people depended on bread lines and soup kitchens.

Both were places where people could go to get free food, such as watery soup and a piece of bread. Some free dinners were sponsored by churches and community groups and others were made available by companies. William Randolph Hearst, who owned many newspapers, set up two bread lines at opposite ends of Times Square in New York City.

People would get into the long, snaking lines hours before the bread line opened, just to get a cup of soup and some bread.

In some parts of the country, away from cities, there might not even be a soup kitchen. In places such as the Appalachian Mountains, people lived on dandelions, pokeweed, blackberries, and anything else they could forage from nature. Some relied on the help of neighbors. Others were reduced to stealing food in order to feed themselves and their families.

People were so desperate for shelter that some even flattened hundreds of tin cans and nailed them to boards to make shelters.

African Americans were segregated in supposedly "separate but equal" schools, restaurants, and public transportation. In most cases, this actually meant separate but unequal and of inferior quality.

The last resort was often scavenging for food in garbage cans and dumps. A woman named Louise Armstrong remembered an incident she saw in Chicago in 1932.

> One vivid, gruesome moment of those dark days we shall never forget. We saw a crowd of some fifty men fighting over a barrel of garbage which had been set outside the back door of a restaurant. American Citizens fighting for scraps of food like animals!

AFRICAN AMERICANS AND RACE RELATIONS

The Great Depression was a time of difficulty for almost everyone, but African Americans were hit the hardest. In some places, unemployment among African Americans was as high as 50 percent, and many whites also called for them to be fired to free up jobs for white workers. This led to more racial violence, such as lynchings. Racial segregation and discrimination increased with more Jim Crow laws, which systematically restricted the civil rights of blacks.

An African American worker receives a paycheck from the WPA

photo credit: U.S. National Archives

When President Roosevelt was elected, he encouraged the inclusion of African Americans in the White House and in his administration. This brought many of them into the Democratic Party. But the reality was that in his new programs for housing and employment, there was still discrimination against African Americans. Some began referring to the New Deal, which was Roosevelt's solution to the Great Depression, as the "Raw Deal," because it did not do enough to help them.

However, many of the New Deal programs offered opportunities to African Americans. The Works Progress Administration (WPA), the program that created many new jobs for people, gave hundreds of thousands of African Americans the opportunity to find work and showcase their talents.

TIME FOR A CHANGE

In 1932, the country was three years into the Great Depression and losing hope. It was also a presidential election year. Under President Hoover, the government had done little to help people. It was time for a change.

Roosevelt accepted the nomination of the Democratic Party with the words, "I pledge you, I pledge myself, to a new deal for the American people." After traveling all over the country to talk to people, Roosevelt beat Herbert Hoover by a landslide.

Roosevelt took office in March 1933. The economy had gotten worse and worse, until many people feared that it would collapse completely. Banks were closing every day. People who had gold were hoarding it. Most Americans felt hopeless. But in his inaugural speech, the new president said, "This nation asks for action, and action now. We must act quickly." And he would.

The media quickly pounced on the words "new deal." Soon, this phrase came to represent the policies that Roosevelt put into effect so that the government could begin to help the American people.

KEY QUESTIONS

- Did President Hoover make good choices while he was president? Would the 1930s have been different if he'd been more active in helping the American people?

- If you had lived during the Great Depression, would you rather live in the city or the country? Why?

- Can you think of examples from your own time when many people had to move because they needed food and shelter?

COOKING 1930S STYLE

During the Great Depression, families often had to be as frugal as possible when preparing meals. Try these Depression-era recipes. Think about why these recipes are symbolic of cooking during the Great Depression. Is either or both something you would eat today?

Hoover Stew

- macaroni
- hot dogs
- canned whole tomatoes
- canned corn or beans, such as chickpeas or white beans

- **Cook the macaroni according to the instructions on the box.** While it cooks, slice the hot dogs into very thin "coins."

- **Open the cans of tomatoes and the can of corn or beans, but do not drain.** Combine the contents of the cans and the hot dog slices in a large pot, and bring to a simmer. Break up the tomatoes into small chunks as the mixture heats.

- **Drain the macaroni when it is barely tender.** Reserve the cooking water to add to the pot, if the tomato-hot dog mixture seems to be too dry.

- **Add the macaroni and continue simmering.** Your Hoover Stew is done when all of the ingredients are thoroughly heated and the hot dogs are cooked.

VOCAB LAB

Write down what you think each word means: **capitalist**, **welfare**, **shantytowns**, **bread line**, **forage**, **nomination**, **civil rights**, **discrimination**, **hoarding**, and **inaugural.**

Compare your definitions with those of your friends or classmates. Did you all come up with the same meanings? Turn to the text and glossary if you need help.

MORE 1930S SLANG

City juice, dog soup: a glass of water

Copper: policeman

Dead hoofer, cement mixer: a bad dancer

Chocolate Depression Cake

- 3 cups flour
- 2 cups sugar
- pinch salt
- 2 teaspoons baking soda
- 10 level tablespoons unsweetened cocoa
- 2 teaspoons vanilla
- ¾ cup vegetable oil
- 2 tablespoons vinegar
- 2 cups cold water

- **Stir dry ingredients into a large mixing bowl.** Add remaining ingredients and mix with a large spoon until smooth. Spoon into a greased and floured 13-by-9-by-2-inch baking pan.

- **Bake at 350 degrees Fahrenheit for 30 minutes.**

ARE YOU SURE WE CAN'T PUT FROSTING ON IT?

To investigate more, create your own Great Depression meal. Use inexpensive ingredients that are readily available. Can you calculate how much it costs to feed your family this meal? Can you stretch it to make two meals?

LET'S TRADE

One method that people used to cope during the Great Depression, when they had very little actual cash, was to barter instead of buy. A doctor might be paid in potatoes or chickens by a farmer with no cash. A seamstress might trade clothing for food from a family with a big garden. Groups of people formed cooperatives, where everyone could exchange what they had for what they needed. Try the bartering system in your classroom or with a group of friends.

- **Agree on an approximate value for items to be bartered, such as $5.** Every person in the group or classroom brings an item from home that they already own that's worth about that amount. They will NOT get the item back. Is it easy or hard to find something to barter?

- **On bartering day, the group sits around a table, each person with their item in front of them.** Go around the circle as each member offers to trade their item for that of another member. Should members have to accept the trade? After the circle is complete, members can make any additional bartering that they want with anyone they want.

- **As a group, discuss whether the bartering system was a success.** Did anyone get something they really wanted in exchange for an item they had but didn't need? Did the system seem fair?

To investigate more, try this bartering activity with tasks or jobs instead of items. How difficult is it to assign equal values to these? How can you make it fair? Alternatively, is it possible to exchange objects or items for tasks or jobs? How would you best organize an ongoing system of bartering?

WORDS TO ELECT A PRESIDENT

Presidential elections have always made use of campaign slogans. They help the public remember something positive about a candidate or something negative about an opponent.

- **What makes a good campaign slogan?** Should it be catchy? Will it work well on buttons and bumper stickers? Is it memorable? Will it be clearly recalled as belonging to that candidate when the voter gets to the polls and thinks about the slogans they've heard?

- **Try creating several new campaign slogans for Herbert Hoover and Franklin Roosevelt.** Your slogans should talk about the candidate's strengths and also point out their opponent's weaknesses.

- **Design campaign buttons or posters using your slogans.** Display your work in your classroom and have students vote on the one they think is most effective.

To investigate more, is there a school election taking place in your school? Either create a campaign slogan for your favorite candidate or research the slogans being used by all student candidates and evaluate which ones are effective and which are not. Do they convey truthfully the candidate's position? Can they be taken seriously, or do they seem unrealistic? How do they affect your perceptions of the candidate's qualifications for the position they are seeking?

1930s SLOGANS

Some of Franklin Roosevelt's campaign slogans included, "Happy days are here again," "Remember Hoover," "Better a Third Term," and, during WWII, "Don't swap horses in midstream" and "We are going to win this war . . . and the peace that follows."

In 1936, presidential candidate Alfred M. Landon used slogans to protest Roosevelt and his New Deal, such as "Defeat the New Deal and Its Reckless Spending" and "Let's Get Another Deck." In 1940, candidate Wendell Willkie's slogans included, "Roosevelt for Ex-President" and "Win with Willkie."

Chapter 3 ▶
A New
Deal

What did the newly elected President Roosevelt do to help the country?

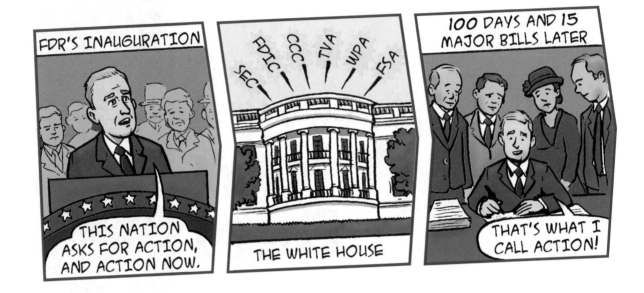

Roosevelt immediately began implementing programs to help Americans. These were called his "New Deal," because many of them were things that had never been tried in America before.

When Franklin Roosevelt was elected president, he knew that the government had to act quickly. Americans were suffering. Many of them were jobless, homeless, and hungry. The first 100 days of Roosevelt's administration came to be called "The Hundred Days" because he was so busy.

First, the new president called Congress back from vacation so that it could quickly approve legislation and started implementing new laws and programs. All of a sudden, people felt as though the government was unleashing new measures designed to help the country. As Roosevelt said, "It is common sense to take a method and try it. If it fails, admit it frankly and try another. But above all, try something."

A NEW DEAL AND NEW IDEAS

One reason Roosevelt's ideas were referred to as the New Deal was because they were very different from the way things had been done before in this country.

Suddenly, some of the old policies that seemed unchangeable and often cruel were being changed. Some of the old ways of doing things included child labor, where children often worked long hours in unsafe working conditions, and no government help for the sick or elderly. Others were the unregulated banks and an unregulated stock market, as well as long work hours at low wages. Who did many of these old ways of doing things benefit? Who did they hurt?

Roosevelt's ideas weren't really new. They were progressive ideas that had been tried in Europe for many years and were now coming to the United States.

> Until now, the government had stubbornly refused to involve itself in the social welfare of its citizens, but Roosevelt changed that with his New Deal programs.

Roosevelt also changed who held power in the government. Previously, most of the country was run by one group of people. These were wealthy, white men of the aristocratic and privileged part of American society. This kind of power excluded many Americans, such as women, minorities, and those from other cultural backgrounds. Roosevelt appointed people with talent and ability to his government, regardless of their background, class, color, or religion.

This was not a popular decision. Roosevelt himself was from this wealthy upper-class group, and many of his peers called him a traitor to his class. Many businessmen also hated Roosevelt because many of his programs added costs and regulations where there had not been any before.

1930s FACTOID

Roosevelt's most famous quote from this period of time was, "The only thing we have to fear is fear itself."

SPEECH! SPEECH!

Franklin Roosevelt gave a rousing speech for his inaugural address that many people found both hopeful and inspiring. Listen to his speech. Find inaugural speeches for other U.S. presidents, such as President Robert Kennedy, President Ronald Reagan, and President Barack Obama. Do they sound different? How? Do you think people would be inspired by President Roosevelt's speech if it were given today?

Roosevelt inaugural speech

Instead of the government working solely to create an atmosphere that was good for business, it was now concerned with helping the workers who made those businesses run. The government was spending money on helping working people instead of just helping businesses.

STARTING WITH BANKS

Just days after his inauguration, the president declared that on March 6, all of the banks in the country would be closed for the day. This was an effort to stop people from panicking and withdrawing their money. The bank closure also meant that no transactions could take place, not even among businesses, unless authorized by the president and the secretary of the treasury. This order meant that the country's gold reserves could not be exported either. Already, much of the country's gold reserves had been depleted by foreign investments.

On March 9, Congress passed the Emergency Banking Act of 1933. It was the first of Roosevelt's many laws and regulations, and one of the most successful. The Emergency Banking Act of 1933 did many things. It authorized the president to keep doing what he had done on March 6, which was to close banks and prevent the exporting of gold. The law also put new regulations in place for how banks were run, set the price for gold and silver, and provided investment funds for qualified banks by having the government purchase bank stock.

The law gave the U.S. Department of the Treasury the ability to call in all gold and gold certificates being held in private hands and exchange them for paper currency. Many people had been hoarding gold because of the bank panics and failures. When the banks reopened on March 13, they would be carefully controlled to keep public deposits safe and prevent more panic.

> The Banking Act worked.
> By March 15, 1933, deposits exceeded
> withdrawals across the country.

People took cash, gold, and gold certificates from hiding places in their homes and deposited them in banks again. There was so much cash and gold being brought in that many banks had to post extra guards to protect it. As a result of the Emergency Banking Act, the reopened banks were once again solvent.

Banking itself was regulated. The creation of the Federal Deposit Insurance Corporation (FDIC) guaranteed that the deposits people made would still be available to them even if their banks failed. All deposits up to $250,000 are insured by the federal government under this law. The FDIC still exists today.

President Roosevelt also took the United States off the gold standard. The gold standard was a system where all currency was backed in gold. This meant that if someone took a $20 bill to the bank, they could demand 20 dollars' worth of gold. Creditors could also demand payment in gold.

By going off the gold standard, the federal government would actually have more gold in its reserves and could use it to issue more paper currency, which would benefit the economy.

Eleanor Roosevelt, 1932

photo credit: Library of Congress

On April 5, 1933, Roosevelt ordered that all gold bullion, gold coins, and gold certificates worth more than $100 be turned in for other types of money. By April 19, it was official—the United States had gone off the gold standard, which had backed its currency since 1900. As a result, more money was issued and inflation boosted the economy, so prices rose.

ELEANOR ROOSEVELT

Franklin Roosevelt and his wife, Eleanor, are considered one of the best political partnerships to have lived the White House. Roosevelt may have been president, but Eleanor was a direct link to the people. She visited coal mines and soup kitchens and factories, and told the president what she had seen and heard. No one was ever sure when she might show up at a public meeting or workplace, and the Secret Service gave her the code name "Rover."

She was also a successful public speaker, radio broadcast personality, and writer, with her own newspaper column titled "My Day." She wrote books, as well as magazine articles for many different publications. Eleanor monitored letters sent to the president and informed him when they needed a response. She also encouraged Americans to write to her directly, and she ultimately received hundreds of thousands of letters.

Early in her husband's term as president, Eleanor Roosevelt established the practice of holding her own press conferences about breaking news, White House administration activities, and social programs. There were times that the president's media office actually preferred to have her announce breaking news because of her rapport with the public.

> Another interesting feature of Eleanor Roosevelt's press conferences was her refusal to allow any male reporters.

Any news organization that wanted to report on her press conferences had to have a female reporter to attend them. This helped further the role of women in professional journalism.

Eleanor Roosevelt supported the needy and the rights of women and minorities, as well as worked for social justice and world peace. After the advent of the New Deal programs, she often toured the country to check on the progress of these programs. She served as First Lady through a period of time that included two traumatic national events: the Great Depression and World War II. Roosevelt is remembered as one of the most outstanding women of the twentieth century.

PUTTING PEOPLE BACK TO WORK

In February 1933, there were still between 12 million and 14 million Americans out of work. Relief funds from cities and states, as well as some federal funds, were quickly running out. Drastic action was needed.

In March 1933, the president asked Congress for two immediate things. First, he wanted more relief funds, and second, he wanted the establishment of a civilian conservation corps. The conservation corps could be used for simple work that wouldn't replace work done by people in existing jobs.

According to President Roosevelt, "The vast majority of unemployed Americans, who are now walking the streets and receiving private or public relief, would infinitely prefer to work." By April 5, Congress had approved the bill authorizing the Civilian Conservation Corps (CCC).

The CCC provided jobs to a specific part of the population. These were young men between the ages of 18 and 25 who were no longer in school, who were unemployed, and whose families were receiving relief. In exchange for their work, they received room and board for a year as well as $30 a month, although $25 of this went straight to their families. The men worked on public lands building roads, parks, beaches, trails, and campgrounds. Many of these improvements are still used today.

> They also planted trees and fought forest fires. By July 1933, there were 1,500 CCC camps in place with more than 250,000 men working.

The Emergency Banking Act and the creation of the Civilian Conservation Corps were just two of the programs created early in Roosevelt's presidency that directly helped the American people. There were many more.

The WPA also put people to work doing everything from building highways and clearing slums to producing regional guidebooks. Writers working for the WPA created oral histories and artists made murals and sculptures for public areas.

1930s

Through the WPA, communities that had never before hosted much in the way of the arts now saw live theater and concerts.

The Federal Art Project (FAP), one of the programs instituted under the WPA, created jobs for more than 5,000 artists who created more than 225,000 works of art. Many examples of this art can still be seen in the remnants of the post office murals that were painted by FAP artists. Some were destroyed during remodeling, but many more still exist as lasting reminders of the contributions made by WPA projects.

> The WPA was one of Roosevelt's most successful programs, giving jobs to 8.5 million people during four years.

The Securities and Exchange Commission (SEC) was formed to regulate the stock market. The Public Works Administration (PWA) employed more Americans and built many structures, such as the Lincoln Tunnel in New York City and the road that links mainland Florida with Key West.

President Hoover had believed in keeping government out of citizens' lives at all costs, but Roosevelt's programs made the government an active part of Americans' lives and a support system for them.

Many of these programs, such as the Social Security Act, still exist as part of everyday American life. Evidence of others, including the WPA, can still be seen today all over the country.

IT'S A GOOD START, BUT THERE'S JUST SO MUCH LEFT TO DO.

A STUMBLING BLOCK TO THE PESSIMIST IS A STEPPING STONE TO THE OPTIMIST.

The Tennessee Valley Authority (TVA) started out as an experiment in regional planning but ended up producing electrical power. The Social Security Act created pensions for the elderly and unemployment benefits, as well as welfare for the elderly, children, and the handicapped.

The New Deal also supported organized labor through the 1935 National Labor Relations Act, which encouraged collective bargaining and protected the rights of employees and employers. By the end of the decade, almost 9 million workers belonged to labor unions, which worked to increase wages, reduce hours, and give workers a voice in setting working conditions. This had a great long-term impact on the living standards of working Americans.

Roosevelt also established the National Recovery Administration to help America recover from the Depression. The administration was given the power to work with business and industry to establish codes to set prices and fair practices.

By 1936, Franklin D. Roosevelt's New Deal had created many solid programs and measures designed to help the average American suffering from the effects of the Great Depression. But there was a larger tragedy at work during the 1930s, one that was not related to bank failures and stock prices. This one would lend the era one of its most enduring nicknames—the Dirty Thirties.

KEY QUESTIONS

- How were Herbert Hoover's presidency and Franklin Roosevelt's presidency different? Were there any similarities?
- The WPA put writers and artists to work as well as tradesmen. Why? How did this benefit society as a whole?

THE WPA

One of the most successful projects of the WPA was the creation of the Federal Writers Project and the production of a series of travel guides to different states and regions of the United States.

* **Research the WPA travel guides, either online or by visiting a local library to see copies of these guides.** How is the information presented? What is the writer's tone? How are illustrations and photographs used in these guides?

* **Research your own city or town and write your own WPA-style travel guide to your local area.** Be sure to cover the same categories that the original guides did, such as places to eat and hometown cuisine, scenic drives, historic sites, and parks. Visit your local Chamber of Commerce or tourist office to get additional information. What is special about your community? Are there any undiscovered gems that some people might overlook or might not know about?

* **Create a 10-page booklet guide to your area.** Use written passages, photos, illustrations, and maps. Make it as appealing as possible.

> To investigate more, find out if your city or town has its own guide for tourists and visitors. Can your completed WPA-style booklet be used as a visitor's guide for your community?

WPA MURALS

You can see some of the WPA murals by going to this site and searching for WPA murals. Can you spot any common themes?

PS

WPA Murals

VOCAB LAB

Write down what you think each word means: **New Deal**, **progressive**, **social welfare**, **aristocratic**, **currency**, and **inflation.**

Compare your definitions with those of your friends or classmates. Did you all come up with the same meanings? Turn to the text and glossary if you need help.

MAKE YOUR OWN DAM

Two projects that provided employment during the Great Depression were the construction of the Hoover Dam and the dam projects created by the Tennessee Valley Authority.

There are four different types of dams: embankment, gravity, arch, and buttress. Engineers decide which type of dam to use by determining the force of the water that will be pushing against the dam, the weight of the dam itself, and outside forces such as waves and earthquake potential. Research each of these dam types and then try building an example of each one. This activity can be done alone or as part of a group, with each group building one type of dam.

You might find this website helpful in your research.

dam design students embankment gravity arch buttress

- **Make four landscape tubs by cutting one side off each of the four containers.** For each type of dam, create a design. This should include a drawing of the tub, the idea for the dam, and dimensions of key features, such as the tub, dam length, and dam thickness

- **Use the materials to build each type of dam.** Remember the key concepts from each dam!

- **For testing, place the entire model into a waterproof bin.** Fill the containers for each dam with water to test its force on the dam. Wait one minute and record your observations. How is it working? Are there any leaks? Is the dam able to withstand the force of the water?

- **Did one type of dam work better than others?** How can you explain why one worked well or didn't work very well?

To investigate more, think about each kind of dam. How could you redesign each type to be more effective? Are there other materials that you could use? Are there different building techniques that would strengthen your dam?

Ideas for Supplies ▼

- large waterproof bins to catch spilled water
- small disposable plastic containers
- coarse sand such as tube sand or sand for concrete
- plastic wrap
- modeling clay
- small dominoes or wood
- dowel, straws, or popsicle sticks

LETTERS TO ELEANOR

During the Great Depression, thousands of children wrote letters to First Lady Eleanor Roosevelt. They asked for things such as money, jobs, clothing, and small luxuries that their parents could not afford to buy for them.

* **Research the letters that children actually wrote.** What are some of the common themes that you notice in these letters?

    letters Eleanor Roosevelt

* **Now imagine that you are a child during the Great Depression.** Write a letter to Mrs. Roosevelt as if you were:

    * A young girl whose parents can't afford food for the family;

    * A young boy whose father just lost his job; and

    * A high school student who will have to drop out of school and get a job to help support the family.

> To investigate more, research Mrs. Roosevelt's response to the letters she received, in terms of programs and agencies specifically intended to help kids during this time. Write a response from the First Lady to one of the children whose letter you wrote. How would you offer hope to the child?

Chapter 4 ▶
A Dusty Disaster

What was the
Dust Bowl and how
did it happen?

The Dust Bowl refers to the part of the country that suffered from devastating droughts and dust storms during the 1930s. The dust storms were so severe that farmers could no longer grow crops and many people were forced to leave the area and their homes.

As if economic problems weren't bad enough in the 1930s, the environment also seemed to turn against many Americans. People who lived in the Great Plains and the Southwest were hurt the most, especially those in Texas, Kansas, Colorado, New Mexico, and the Panhandle region of Oklahoma. The weather events that took place there affected the entire country and made life extremely difficult for many people.

WIND, HEAT, AND NO WATER

Have you ever visited the Great Plains? This region is one of extreme weather. The wind blows constantly and both the heat and the cold can reach extreme temperatures. Rainfall can be unpredictable. Left alone, the plains create a carpet of thick, tough grasses that have long, tangled roots anchoring them into the soil. This creates a mat of sod that is good at holding rainwater.

> The grasses rooted in this sod also prevent the topsoil from blowing away in the strong winds.

When there is a normal amount of rain, the Great Plains can be a good place for farming. After the Civil War, when the U.S. government passed the Homestead Act, settlers could buy their own land in the Great Plains region by simply paying a $10 fee and living on the land for five years. These settlers came to the region during a period of time when rainfall was plentiful, and they turned up the sod with their plows and planted crops.

Wheat, corn, and oats flourished and farmers plowed up more and more land. These crops were grown and harvested every year, unlike the grasses that had grown on the prairie for so long. Called "cash crops" because they were so lucrative, wheat, corn, and oats could not survive drought and extreme heat because their root systems were so shallow.

BEFORE THE DROUGHT

As farm crop prices began to fall during the 1920s, farmers needed to produce more and more just to make ends meet. They plowed up even more sod and planted even more shallow-rooted cash crops.

A farmer harvesting his wheat field in Idaho in the 1920s

photo credit: waterarchives.org

In his famous novel, *The Grapes of Wrath*, author John Steinbeck tells the story of the Joad family, who were forced to leave their Oklahoma farm and travel to California hoping for work and a better life. Although it is a fictional story, Steinbeck had worked as a newspaper reporter and actually interviewed some of the "Okie" families who experienced what the Joads did.

Most of the farmers had never experienced a drought on the Great Plains and they never considered that the wonderful growing conditions would end. By the end of the 1920s, even more of the grasslands had become farm fields in what became known as "The Great Plow-Up." No one ever imagined that the fertile, deep, rich soil of the plains could be exhausted or abused.

But 1930 saw the beginning of a severe drought that affected the entire country. In the eastern United States, crops dried up in the fields and farmers faced foreclosure of their farms and homes. In 1931, the drought shifted to the Great Plains. Not only was there no rain, but temperatures soared to levels that people had never seen before. In some places, the temperature reached as high as 118 degrees and stayed at that level for days. The area was known as the Dust Bowl.

The heat and lack of water affected not only people and crops. These hot, dry conditions were perfect for hatching grasshoppers, which swarmed in huge numbers. Grasshoppers ate everything they could find, including crops, tool handles, and even the paint off of houses.

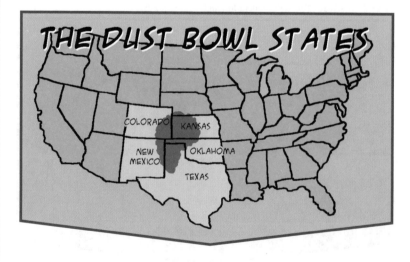

THE DUST BOWL STATES

COLORADO KANSAS
NEW MEXICO OKLAHOMA
TEXAS

But the very worst results of the drought were dust storms. These were actually a natural occurrence on the plains, where loose soil was occasionally swept away in huge dark clouds and deposited elsewhere. Most early settlers accepted these storms as normal inconveniences to just wait out as they might wait out a blizzard. But the dust storms of the 1930s were something else entirely.

Because so much of the earth had been plowed up for farming, the system of sod and deeply rooted grasses that kept the soil in place had been destroyed. So, these dust storms were larger and more intense than anything experienced before.

> Thanks to the work of humans and their method of farming, the dust storms became a natural disaster.

THE DIRTY THIRTIES

The huge dust storms that gave the 1930s its nickname started in 1933. One storm in May 1934 was so extreme that it carried away 350 million tons of topsoil. Tons of dust created a gritty haze as far away as Chicago and New York, creating a dim twilight. Even out at sea, sailors could write their names in the dust that settled on the decks of their ships.

One of the biggest, most frightening dust storms took place on April 14, 1935. This was a day called "Black Sunday." The storm was a thousand miles wide and traveled about 1,500 miles in two days.

DUST BOWL

You can see pictures and watch video footage of the 1930s dust storms. How did people deal with these huge clouds of dust? What do you think it felt like to live in the Dust Bowl?

Dust Bowl video archives

1930s FACTOID

Jackrabbits were another species, along with grasshoppers, that managed to thrive in the Dust Bowl. Whatever managed to grow in the fields was eaten quickly by the hundreds of thousands of rabbits that hopped in the wild.

A.D. Kirk, a man from Texas, described what the storm looked like as it approached his town.

I noticed a low dark line of what I first thought was a cloud along the northern horizon. It made no sense. There was not a cloud in the sky. As I watched, it got taller and spread from the west to the east horizon. . . . The front of the cloud was a rolling, tumbling, boiling mass of dust and dirt about two hundred feet high, almost vertical, and as black as an Angus bull. It came across the prairie like a two-hundred-foot-high tidal wave, pushed along by a sixty-mile-per-hour wind. When it got to a house or power pole or any other object, the house or whatever disappeared.

The monster dust storms not only coated everything, inside and outside, with layers of grit and dust, but they created a health hazard as well. Some doctors felt that the dust storms created a new form of respiratory disease as dust collected in people's lungs. The death rate from respiratory diseases such as bronchitis rose, as well as the death rates of those already suffering from asthma or tuberculosis.

[
Many people became sick with silicosis, a lung disease caused by inhaling dust. The dust acted like glass, slowly shredding the lungs.
]

Farm animals also suffered. Horses and mules could be protected a little by muzzling them with bags or grain sacks, but wild cattle out on the range could not be helped. The dust collected on the rims of their eyes, mixing with tears to create a mud that cemented their eyes together and blinded them.

The dust from the storms was inescapable. A woman in Garden City, Kansas, described what it was like to experience a dust storm.

> All we could do about it was just sit in our dusty chairs, gaze at each other through the fog that filled the room and watch the fog settle slowly and silently, covering everything—including ourselves—in a thick, brownish-gray blanket . . . The door and windows were all shut tightly, yet those tiny particles seemed to seep through the very walls. It got into cupboards and clothes closets . . . our hair was gray and stiff and we ground dirt between our teeth.

As the dust storms worsened and farming was no longer possible, many people had no choice but to leave their farms and homes. They went looking for a better life elsewhere.

1930s FACTOID

Agricultural migrants who left their farms in search of a new life were sometimes called "Okies," even though only a fifth of them were from Oklahoma.

HITTING THE ROAD

Unable to farm and often in debt, individuals and families left the Dust Bowl region and headed out, often toward California. By 1940, more than 2.5 million people had left the regions affected by the dust storms, and 10 percent of those had gone to California.

Why California? Rumors abounded that there was plenty of work there harvesting crops and that no one ever went hungry because people could simply help themselves to fruits and vegetables growing in lush orchards and fields. They also saw advertisements nailed to trees and fence posts that called for workers to harvest crops in California. The ads promised high wages and immediate work.

Some families packed up their belongings in overloaded, ramshackle vehicles and headed out. They were called "tin can tourists" and usually camped by the side of the road, doing laundry and washing in streams. The "tourists" stopped only for gas or oil or to let their car radiator cool off.

> With luck, no breakdowns, and about $10 worth of gasoline, they might make it from Oklahoma to California in three or four days.

People who were completely broke and traveling on their own either hitchhiked or rode illegally in boxcars on trains. These travelers were known as hoboes. Hoboes stayed alive by begging for food or doing a few odd jobs in exchange for a meal wherever they were. They often slept in camps near railroad tracks, where they could hope to catch a train to a new place.

Many hoboes were treated harshly by railroad officials whose job it was to keep hoboes from riding the trains. According to the Interstate Commerce Commission, during the years from 1929 to 1939, almost 25,000 people trespassing on railroad property were killed and another 27,000 were injured. Many were killed in accidents as they got on and off moving trains. It is estimated that 250,000 teens, some as young as 13, were among those traveling by rail on their own.

Eric Sevareid, a 20-year-old hobo, described life as a hobo and living in the encampments by the railroads.

> Tens of thousands of American men, women, and children, white, black, brown, and yellow, who inhabit the "jungle," eat from blackened tin cans, find warmth at night in the boxcars, take the sun by day on the flatcars, steal one day, beg with cap in hand the next, fight with fists and often razors . . . wander from town to town, anxious for the next place, tired of it in a day, fretting to be gone again, happy only when the wheels are clicking under them, the telephone poles slipping by.

Boy hopping freight train, 1940

photo credit: Library of Congress, Prints & Photographs Division, FSA/OWI Collection

DOROTHEA LANGE

Photographer Dorothea Lange created a series of photographs of migrant families heading for California as a result of the Dust Bowl. She was hired by the Farm Security Administration to document the plight of migrants and farmers, and took thousands of photographs between 1935 and 1943. Many of these images were used in newspapers and magazines, as well as being shown to politicians to persuade the government to step in and help these people. Lange's photographs are some of the most poignant and lasting images of the Great Depression. You can view a selection of her images. What do the pictures make you think of? What do they make you feel?

PBS
Dorothea Lange
biography
gallery

As many teens and adults hit the road and became hoboes, they developed a vocabulary of signs that they could use to communicate with each other. These signs usually conveyed information such as whether a house was willing to give out food or if the family there was friendly. Other important information could be if a telephone was available, if someone in the family slept during the day, or whether there were any dangers or reasons to avoid a particular house.

> The people who lived in homes described with hobo signs may not have been aware that they had been marked as a good place to beg or a good place to avoid.

WHAT STEINBECK SAYS

Author John Steinbeck witnessed the effect of the Great Depression on U.S. citizens firsthand, and many of his books feature people and families down on their luck. You can listen to a video interview with Steinbeck in which he discusses *The Grapes of Wrath*.

🔍 Steinbeck interview Grapes of Wrath

TEN MEN FOR EVERY JOB

Those who struggled to leave the Dust Bowl region rarely found the jobs they had been told awaited them in California. Many California towns had signs at their borders that read, "NO JOBS HERE! IF YOU ARE LOOKING FOR WORK—KEEP OUT! 10 MEN FOR EVERY JOB!" Towns were afraid that they would have to provide relief to migrant families who ended up in their communities.

Officials were stationed at city and town limits to turn back hitchhikers and migrants. Some even enacted laws to keep migrants out, although they would later be overturned as unconstitutional—Americans had the right to travel anywhere they wanted to in their own country.

When there was no work to be found, migrant families quickly ran out of money for food or even to buy gas and travel somewhere else. Many camped wherever they could. In many cases, families were starving, even though they were in a state with one of the richest agricultural industries.

Farms often produced surplus crops, but the owners would sometimes pour oil on extra produce and burn it. This was a way to decrease the amount of product available, which inflated the price of the product. They also wanted to prevent migrants from eating the extra and force them to move on. John Steinbeck saw this happen firsthand and called it the "saddest, bitterest thing of all."

[The federal government finally built 10 farm-labor camps in California where migrant families could live until they found work.]

Families lived in one-room cabins or in tents on wooden platforms, paying $1 a week for rent or working off their rent doing maintenance around the camp. There was food available and children could often go to school.

LESSONS LEARNED?

The Dust Bowl had the immediate effect of driving many farmers into poverty and out of their homes for good. The government responded by forming the Soil Conservation Service in 1935. Its purpose was to teach farmers how to plant grass and trees to anchor down the soil. They learned how to plow and terrace their land in ways that would hold water better than flat fields. Farmers also learned to leave portions of their land unplanted so it could rest and regenerate.

MORE 1930s SLANG

Dizzy with a dame: being in love with a woman

Stems, pins, gams: legs

Eggs in coffee: when something runs smoothly

1930s FACTOID

Those advertisements promising immediate work in California were no longer true, as the California growers had advertised for more workers than they actually needed. Migrant workers, desperate for jobs, would work for very low wages.

The government purchased more than 11 million acres of poor land to keep it out of use and in recovery.

These measures worked, and by 1941, a lot of the land was rehabilitated. Unfortunately, farmers would repeat some of the same mistakes during World War II when grain prices rose. Another drought in the 1950s led the government to start paying farmers to leave their land planted in grass.

The 1930s were a time of extreme hardship for many people. But everyday life also continued. And there was plenty going on. What was it like to live during that time?

KEY QUESTIONS

- Why did the farmers destroy the very thing they relied on for their livelihood—the soil?
- What responsibility does a state government have to help people who travel there from other states in hopes of finding work?
- Were agricultural owners right to destroy surplus food so migrants would move on? Why or why not?

HOT AND DRY

The Dust Bowl happened partly because of poor agricultural practices and partly because of drought and heat.

- **Research the weather data from the 1930s.** How much land in the Dust Bowl region was under cultivation at this time?

- **Create a map that shows the areas where land had been plowed up for agriculture.** How does this compare to the regions most severely affected by the Dust Bowl? Create an accompanying graph showing the temperatures and rainfall amounts for each year in the 1930s.

- **Now create a map showing the areas of the Dust Bowl region that had been plowed up for agriculture by 1920.** What difference is there between this map and the 1930s map? Create a graph showing how much land was being used for agriculture in 1920 and 1930. What were temperatures and rainfalls like in 1920? Create a graph showing temperatures and rainfalls in 1920 and in 1930.

> To investigate more, create a map showing the areas of the Dust Bowl region that had been plowed up for agriculture by 1960. What difference is there between this map and the 1930s map? Create a graph showing how much land was being used for agriculture in 1920, 1930, and 1960. What were temperatures and rainfalls like in the 1950s? Create a graph showing temperatures and rainfalls during the different decades.

WOODY GUTHRIE

As folksinger Woody Guthrie said in his song "Great Storm Disaster":

We loaded our jalopies and piled our families in,

We rattled down that highway to never come back again.

Inquire & Investigate

ON THE ROAD

What would it be like to live through the Dust Bowl and to lose your farm? What would you and your family do?

- **Imagine that you are the child of an Okie family fleeing the Dust Bowl area of Oklahoma and traveling toward California in hopes of finding work.** Research what the circumstances and conditions were like for these children.

- **Write a journal or a series of letters home to a relative.** Describe what is happening and what you are seeing. What are the attitudes toward you of the people you meet? What are the stories you've heard about what California is like? What do you actually find when you get there?

- **Write another letter home as if you were a teen traveling around the country by hopping illegal rides on freight trains.** What are you seeing and experiencing? What dangers do you face? Where do you sleep and how do you eat? Make your writing as vivid and descriptive as possible.

> To investigate more, research narratives from actual migrant kids and teens, perhaps as told to writers and photographers from the federal Writer's Project or another WPA program. Compare them to your narrative. Is there anything you missed?

VOCAB LAB

Write down what you think each word means: **respiratory, topsoil, unconstitutional, migrant, terrace,** and **plight.**

Compare your definitions with those of your friends or classmates. Did you all come up with the same meanings? Turn to the text and glossary if you need help.

HOBO SIGNS

During the Great Depression, hoboes had their own system of signs to let each other know about good and bad places to ask for food or lodging, as well as places to avoid.

- **Look at the examples of hobo signs and their meanings here.**

 nsa hobo
signs

- **Imagine that you need to leave signs for your friends or classmates about places in your school that are good for certain things or should be avoided.** For example, what kind of sign would you put on your cafeteria door? On the locker of a friend who is always willing to give you a ride home from school? On a corner of the hallway where it's safe to send a text message or make a call without being caught?

- **Think of the messages you might want to send, and then create a drawing for each one.** Compile your drawings into a mini-"dictionary" of your secret school signs. You can also make up examples of your symbols and have your classmates try to guess what each one might mean.

To investigate more, find out if hobo signs are still being used today. Do today's homeless people have a system for communicating with each other? Is there a link between modern graffiti and hobo signs from the Great Depression era? Do they convey similar messages?

Chapter 5 ▶
Quintuplets, Gangsters, and Monopoly

What was everyday life like during the 1930s?

Life during the 1930s was not all hardship and struggle. People still found ways to have fun. Groundbreaking events took place at home and around the world during this decade.

The 1930s were difficult years in many ways. But it was also a decade when everyday life was changing. The modernization of American life, which had begun in the 1920s, continued despite the terrible economic conditions. Because of the economy, many workers had a five-day workweek for the first time in their lives. On the other hand, lots of people lost faith in the "American dream," where they could work their way up to a solid middle-class lifestyle with a nice house and a car in the driveway. It was a time of shifting attitudes brought on by hard reality.

HOME SWEET HOME

There were many people who were unable to pay their mortgages and they lost their homes during the Great Depression. Others were able to continue living in their houses, but found themselves sheltering relatives who had nowhere else to go after losing their own homes.

In the cities, multiple families and multiple generations sometimes crammed into apartments meant for far fewer people. Because so few people could afford new houses, housing prices fell from an average of $7,145 for a new home in 1930, to only $3,800 in 1939. The average home price in 2014 was $188,900.

Most homes in the 1930s had electric refrigerators, electric or gas stoves, and sometimes even electric washing machines. Electric fans, electric mixers, vacuum cleaners, and clothes dryers were available, but many households could not afford them. Some families had to revert to older ways of doing things if their gas or electric power was shut off due to nonpayment.

[
Lots of people went back to cooking over wood stoves, using hand-crank washing machines, and storing perishable food in iceboxes instead of electric refrigerators.
]

It was common for households to own automobiles in the 1930s. Henry Ford's pioneering assembly-line technology had made cars cheaper and more affordable for the average person. And, despite the economy during the Great Depression, when fewer people were in the market for new cars, the automobile industry developed many innovations that made cars better and more mechanically sound.

Many of the features invented during this time have stayed with cars to this day. These include automatic transmissions, hydraulic brakes, car radios, and more powerful engines, such as the V8. For the first time, trunks were built into the car's body.

1930s FACTOID

Car designs became more stylish. Instead of the square body styles of the early cars, manufacturers developed a rounder, sleeker body style that was more aerodynamic.

Westinghouse vacuum cleaner with attachment kit: $39.95

Philco auto radio: $24.95

Ladies' winter coats: $16

Boys' pants: $1.98

Men's socks: 10 cents

Children's underwear: 49 cents

1936 Ford V8 car: $510

Toothpaste: 27 cents

Bacon: 38 cents per pound

1930s FACTOID

Some designers, including Madeleine Vionnet and Elsa Schiaparelli, designed women's suits to cater to women who were working in offices and business environments.

WHAT'S FASHIONABLE?

Fashion in the 1930s went back to being more conservative than it had been in the Roaring Twenties. At the same time, as Hollywood and celebrities became more popular, fashions imitated some of the glamour and elegance seen on the movie screen.

During the Roaring Twenties, women's fashions were a reflection of a newfound freedom. Women wore shorter skirts, shorter hair, and loose dresses with lower waistlines. They no longer wore corsets, and strived for an ideal body image that was boyish and without curves. Outfits were sometimes outrageous, with fringe and gemstones and feathers.

Fashions in the 1930s, on the other hand, returned to a more natural shape for women. Dresses had longer skirts, but they also accentuated women's natural waistlines and curves.

> Sports and fitness had become more popular, so sports clothes such as tennis clothing and swimming outfits were popular as well.

Evening clothes became more elegant, such as gowns for women that were long and backless. Women's hairstyles also changed from the boyish "bob" cuts of the 1920s to longer curls and waves.

Men's fashions changed too. Suits were designed to make it look as though the wearer had a large torso, with padded shoulders, wide pointed lapels, and tapered sleeves. To save fabric and cost, suits were cut narrower than they had been in the 1920s. Colors became more somber, and included grays, blues, and browns. The trench coat also became popular.

The average working man wore work pants and a jacket with a cap. Beards became less acceptable, but small mustaches were popular. What can we learn by the fashion of the time? What does the fashion of today say about the values of your generation?

PROHIBITION REPEALED!

One major change in the way people entertained themselves in the 1930s was because of the repeal of Prohibition. In 1920, the Eighteenth Amendment to the U.S. Constitution had made it illegal to sell liquor anywhere in the United States. The intention was to limit the negative effects of drinking. Prohibition was supposed to stop people from spending all their money and time in a saloon rather than taking care of their families.

In time, this experiment in limiting alcohol consumption failed. Drinking became even more enticing when it was illegal, and visiting speakeasies, where liquor was sold illegally, became popular entertainment. People could almost always find liquor when they wanted it. Illegal alcohol became a big business for gangsters and bootleggers, who made vast fortunes selling liquor illegally.

Even as many people struggled to fulfill their basic needs, luxuries were being invented to improve daily life.

Some politicians and experts believed that making alcohol legally accessible to people again would help boost the country's sagging morale. It would also help the government treasury.

Journalist Walter Lippmann argued:

> Beer would have a decidedly soothing tendency on the present mental attitude of the working men . . . . It would do a great deal to change their mental attitude on economic conditions . . . . Beer would be a great help in fighting off the mental depression which afflicts great multitudes.

The government, desperately in need of money, saw potential revenue in the return of a federal tax on the sale of liquor. In December 1933, the Twenty-first Amendment was passed, repealing Prohibition. It was now legal to drink again, and yet people actually ended up drinking less than they did during Prohibition!

FUN TIMES

People found many other ways to have fun during the 1930s. Miniature golf became tremendously popular after it was invented in Florida in 1929. It continued to be a popular pastime into the next decade, with courses springing up complete with miniature buildings, bridges, and other obstacles. Sports were popular, too, especially baseball, basketball, boxing, and horse racing.

Many games were invented or became popular again during the thirties. *Monopoly*, a game based on *The Landlord's Game* by Lizzie Magie, was invented in 1935 by Charles Darrow. Darrow made the first sets of *Monopoly* by hand and sold them himself until Parker Brothers began manufacturing and marketing it.

Lizzie Magie patented a game called *The Landlord's Game* in 1904, long before *Monopoly*. It was a real estate and tax game intended to show how the system of rents made money for the rich but impoverished the poor. Magie hoped that children would learn about the unfairness of the rent system from playing the game.

Parker Brothers bought Magie's patent for the *The Landlord's Game* in 1935 for $500 when it started selling *Monopoly*. The company was trying to buy up any similar games on the market. Today, it is generally acknowledged that *Monopoly* was directly inspired by *The Landlord's Game* and wasn't completely invented by Darrow.

Backgammon, an ancient board game, also became popular. Bingo was played frequently, and gambling with cards was popular. The chain letter—a letter promising good luck or wealth to those who pass it on—was also part of this era's entertainment.

There were some unusual pastimes that became fads during this time. One was tree-sitting, and its variation, flagpole-sitting. People would try to break the record for the longest period of time sitting in a tree or sitting in a chair on the top of a flagpole, hoping for publicity and fame.

1930s FACTOID

Chain letters still exist today, although they are now usually sent via email.

MORE 1930s SLANG

G-man: a federal agent

Gobble-pipe: a saxophone

Low down: all the information

Couples taking part in a dance marathon, 1923

11 MINUTES OF REST

Special areas were set up for dance marathon participants, segregated by gender, where they were allowed a brief, 11-minute break. A *Seattle Post-Intelligencer* reporter visited the women's rest area at the 1928 Seattle Armory marathon and wrote:

"Here in the half-light they lie, these sprawling, unconscious forms, their cots side by side, their clothing hung in listless disarray . . . a girl is sprawled, her lips moving in pain, as she moans incoherently, and jerks her hands. Bending over her is a man, her 'trainer' apparently, who massages her swollen feet with some ointment. Beside her, another girl is lying, her mouth open to reveal her gold-crowned molars, while flies crawl across her closed eyes and buzz against her chin."

—Alice Elinor, *Seattle Post-Intelligencer*, August 8, 1928

Another unusual contest was the dance marathon. Couples competed for prize money by dancing for hundreds of hours with only brief periods of rest. Dancing was already a popular pastime, with the advent of new dances such as the jitterbug.

Dance marathons were endurance events! Contestants had to stay in motion almost around the clock. They danced, shuffled, rocked, or sprinted, while spectators paid 25 cents to watch them.

LET US ENTERTAIN YOU

Books were popular entertainment, especially since they could be borrowed for free from local libraries. Bestsellers included *The Good Earth* by Pearl S. Buck, *Goodbye Mr. Chips* and *Lost Horizon* by James Hilton, *Gone With the Wind* by Margaret Mitchell, *Of Mice and Men* and *The Grapes of Wrath* by John Steinbeck, and *The Yearling* by Marjorie Kinnan Rawlings. Have you read any of these? What did you learn about the 1930s?

The 1930s also saw the birth of two famous comic book characters. Superman first appeared in Action Comics #1 in June 1938. Batman, created by artist Bob Kane, appeared in Detective Comics #27 in May 1939.

[Why do you think people were excited to read stories about superheroes during the 1930s?]

Music, movies, and games were also popular in the 1930s. Two enduring movies, *Gone With the Wind* and *The Wizard of Oz*, premiered at this time. Just like today, fans loved movie stars, who included Clark Gable, child star Shirley Temple, Joan Crawford, Will Rogers, and the dance team Fred Astaire and Ginger Rogers.

The 1930s were the golden age of radio, before television came to dominate people's living rooms. At the start of the decade, 12 million Americans owned radios, but by 1939, that number had grown to 28 million. Radio shows such as *Amos 'n' Andy*, *The Lone Ranger*, and *The Shadow* were popular.

> Radios brought entertainment, comedy, music, and news right into American homes, as well as Roosevelt's famous "Fireside Chats," which connected citizens to their president.

The jitterbug was a type of swing dance that remained popular right through the 1950s and spawned several other famous dances, including the Lindy hop, the East Coast Swing, and jive.

CELEBRITIES AND STARS

Despite the Great Depression, or maybe because of it, the 1930s had its share of celebrities and stars. These included sports stars such as Jesse Owens. He was a track and field athlete who won four gold medals in the 1936 Olympics in Germany.

1930s FACTOID

The 1930s was the era of Bonnie and Clyde, "Baby Face" Nelson, Ma Barker, and John Dillinger, who was known as Public Enemy Number 1.

As an African American who was the grandson of slaves, Owens faced discrimination all of his life. His presence at the Olympic Games proved that Hitler's insistence of the superiority of white athletes was false. Hitler had wanted German athletes to dominate the games, to show the resurgence of the Nazi Party, but instead, Owens dominated the track and field events, proving that his race was not inferior.

Another famous sports star was baseball player Joe DiMaggio, who played center field for the New York Yankees. DiMaggio led his team to nine World Series championships, and his 56-game hitting streak still stands as a record.

Other sports stars included Joe Louis, one of the greatest Heavyweight boxers of all time. He was World Heavyweight Champion from 1937 to 1949. One famous sports personality, named Seabiscuit, wasn't even human. Seabiscuit was a champion thoroughbred racehorse who was undersized and did not have a very successful racing career to start with.

> The rise of Seabiscuit to champion status made him a symbol of hope to Americans during the darkness of the Depression.

There were also stars of the silver screen during the 1930s. Shirley Temple was the top box office draw from 1935 to 1938. She was a child star who made her first movie at the age of three. Her many movies included *The Littlest Rebel* and *Curly Top*. Shirley Temple was famous for her hair, which was curled into tight ringlets, as well as her singing and dancing abilities.

Another famous 1930s star was the complete opposite of Shirley Temple. Charlie Chaplin was born into poverty in England in 1889, and lived one of the most famous rags-to-riches stories. He got his start during the era of silent movies. Chaplin often played roles in which he was a tramp wearing a bowler hat and a black tailcoat and a sad expression on his face.

IN THE NEWS

How do you get your news? Many people today read or listen to the news online, but in the 1930s, people accessed the news from radios, newspapers, and the informational newsreels shown before movies.

One of the biggest and most poignant news stories of the decade was the kidnapping of the 20-month-old son of Charles Lindbergh in 1932. Lindberg was an aviation hero who was the first person to fly nonstop across the Atlantic in 1927.

LISTEN TO THE LINDBERGH KIDNAPPING

The Lindbergh kidnapping captured the attention of much of the world. Watch this British newsreel of Hauptmann's trial from 1935. How is this newscast different from what you might find online at sites such as cnn.com or bbc.com? What do you notice about the way the newscaster speaks?

Lindbergh baby reel 2 1935

The world's fair was held in New York in 1939 and again in 1964, but they were very different fairs. In 1939, people were amazed at the potential of the future—television, fashion, robotics, and food. In 1964, the world's fair was dominated by corporations, including Disney, and ideas about the space age. But both were great in their own ways.

THE QUINTS

You can see a video of the Dionne quints here. Is this video different from the television shows featuring unusual families today? Is it similar?

PS

Dionne quints video

The baby was kidnapped from a second-story bedroom. Because Lindbergh was so famous, the entire country watched and listened breathlessly as a huge reward was offered for his return. Six weeks later, the baby's body was found about five miles from his home. After a two-year investigation, a man named Bruno Richard Hauptmann was arrested and convicted of the crime.

In Canada in 1934, Mrs. Oliva Dionne gave birth to quintuplets—five little girls—which was a very rare occurrence! The "quints" were in the news for years, especially after the Canadian government took over their care and exhibited them to the public.

A zeppelin is a large aircraft without wings. It floats because it has bags filled with gas that is lighter than air. During the 1930s, zeppelins were used to transport passengers across the Atlantic Ocean.

[
On May 6, 1937, the German zeppelin *Hindenburg* exploded into flames above Lakehurst, New Jersey.
]

The year 1937 also brought news of flooding along the Ohio River. Record rainfall in January and February resulted in high water levels from Pittsburg, Pennsylvania, to Cairo, Illinois. About 385 people died, a million were left homeless, and property losses reached $500 million, which is about $8 billion in today's money.

Gangsters and mobsters were also in the news. These were outlaws who robbed banks, kidnapped people, and sometimes committed murder. Mobsters were different from gangsters because they operated organized crime rings and generally dealt in larger crimes such as bootlegging, gambling, and prostitution.

TO THE FAIR

An amazing entertainment experience for those who could afford it was the annual world's fair. This was an enormous combination of carnivals and exhibitions that showcased the cultures and achievements of many nations. The world's fair included restaurants, midway attractions, stores, and almost any form of entertainment that could be dreamed of.

World's fairs took place throughout the 1930s in Chicago, San Diego, San Francisco, and Dallas. The New York World's Fair opened on Sunday, April 30, 1939, with the theme, "The World of Tomorrow." It included modern architecture and exhibits featuring some of the newest inventions and innovations.

There is no question that the 1930s were a dark and difficult time for many Americans. But they still found ways to entertain themselves and brighten what was often a drab, penny-pinching existence.

WORLD OF TOMORROW, WORLD OF ALREADY

You can watch a video comparing the two New York world's fairs here.

Time world of tomorrow past

Which would you have rather gone to? You can also see iconic photographs of the 1939 world's fair here.

Atlantic World's Fair 1939

KEY QUESTIONS

- How was the entertainment of the 1930s different from that of the 1920s? How was it different from present times?
- Why were chain letters popular?
- The world's fair was a chance for people to see new innovations and inventions. How do people find out about these things now?

LET'S PLAY BACKGAMMON

One of the most popular games during the Great Depression was backgammon. It became such a fad that stores often could not keep backgammon sets in stock. Now, you can make your own backgammon set and learn how to play.

* **Measure off the playing field on the sheet of cardboard.** You want 12 playing pieces to be able to sit comfortably across the center of the playing field with some space to divide the two sides. This will give you the measurement for the width of the board, about 21 or 22 inches. To find the length of your board, lay 13 playing pieces side-by-side. This will give you enough room for 12 pips (the colored triangular markings on the board), six on each home side, and room in the center for your captured checkers to sit. Your board length should come to around 23 to 24 inches. Once you have determined the size of your playing field, center it on your cardboard and mark off borders. You'll want to have borders of at least 1 or 2 inches.

HINDENBURG DISASTER

Listen to the radio broadcast of the Hindenburg Disaster and see images. Does it make you think of any disasters that have happened in your time?

Hindenburg disaster WLS radio video

- **Begin marking the pips.** Each quadrant of the backgammon board has six pips. Leave space between the left-hand and right-hand quadrants for captured checkers to sit. At the base, pips should be about the same width as the playing pieces. You can have them narrow as sharply or as gradually as you'd like. Keep in mind that on traditional boards, five checkers can sit on one pip, and you will still see the tip of the pip protruding beyond the fifth checker. Use a ruler to keep the pips even and straight.

- **Decide which two colors you will use.** Traditionally, the rightmost pip on the home side of the board (the one facing you) is the lighter color. For example, if you choose red and black for your colors, paint the pip on your right-hand side red, then every other pip moving counter-clockwise from there should be red. The last pip on the right-hand side of the board opposite you will be black. Allow the paint or markers to completely dry.

- **To see a diagram of a backgammon board and to learn how to play, visit the U.S. Backgammon Federation website.**

U.S. Backgammon Federation

To investigate more, organize a family game night and have a backgammon tournament! Why do you think backgammon was such a popular game during the 1930s?

VOCAB LAB 📖

Write down what you think each word means: **bootlegger**, **perishable**, **assembly line**, **revenue**, **mobster**, and **patent**.

Compare your definitions with those of your friends or classmates. Did you all come up with the same meanings? Turn to the text and glossary if you need help.

WHAT'S IN YOUR CLOSET?

Fashions change from year to year and from decade to decade. What people wear can reflect the times and the mood of the population: exuberance, optimism, frugality, gloom. What fashions were popular during the Great Depression and why?

- **Research the clothing that both men and women wore at the time.** What did men wear to the office? What did women wear at home? How did people wear their hair?

- **Create drawings of your own designs for typical 1930s outfits for a man, woman, boy, and girl.** Remember to use fabrics and colors that are appropriate to the era.

- **If you are good at creating your own patterns and sewing, you can make an outfit for a doll or even for yourself in a 1930s style.** Or visit a local thrift store or a relative's attic and see if you can find any vintage 1930s clothing to show to your classmates. Are the clothes comfortable to wear? Do they feel different from your usual clothes?

> To investigate more, research 1930s clothing that people wore for different activities. What would you wear if you wanted to go swimming? How would you dress if you were going to church? What about if you were going to a party?

DANCE, DANCE, DANCE

What kind of music were people listening to in the 1930s? What dances were popular during that time? Research the music of the Great Depression, paying close attention to the music that people listened and danced to.

- **Research what dances were popular at the time.** With a partner, or as a team with several other students, learn one or two of these dances.

- **Find appropriate music from the time to dance to.** Once you have learned the dances, put on a demonstration for your classroom. You can even invite them to learn the dances with you and have a classroom mini-dance. How about holding a dance marathon? You can do it to raise money for a good cause!

To investigate more, think about how people listened to music at home in an era before television and Internet videos. Research popular radio programs of the time that might have played dance music, and create your own short 1930s radio music program complete with vintage music.

LET'S DANCE

Fred Astaire and Ginger Rogers might be Hollywood's most famous dancing pair, appearing in 10 movies together. Audiences loved seeing them smoothly bring complex routines to life on the stage. You can see one of their most famous dances.

Astaire Rogers
dance video

I FEEL RIDICULOUS.

YOU'RE DOING GREAT!

Chapter 6 ▶
Inventing the World of Tomorrow

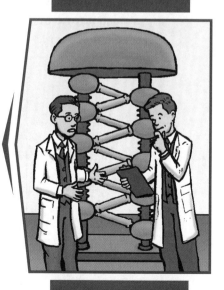

Were any important inventions or scientific discoveries made during the 1930s?

Many of the products we use today, as well as many important technologies, were invented during the 1930s. The decade was also a time of incredible discovery.

The 1930s may have been a time of hardship, unemployment, and general discouragement, but amazing new inventions continued to move the world into the modern age. Many things invented or created during this time are either still in use today or they paved the way to even more modern inventions.

AN AGE OF DISCOVERY

Important new discoveries were made every year during the 1930s. On February 18, 1930, astronomer Clyde W. Tombaugh discovered Pluto from the Lowell Observatory in Flagstaff, Arizona. He had been looking to explain why the orbits of Uranus and Neptune wobbled slightly. The theory was that the wobble happened because of the effect of gravity from a ninth planet. He found it, and on March 13, 1930, announced to the world that Pluto was indeed the ninth planet in our solar system.

In 1925, Vannevar Bush, a faculty member in the electrical engineering department at Massachusetts Institute of Technology (MIT), suggested that one of his graduate students devise a machine to solve difficult equations. Solutions to complex equations were necessary for electrical engineers to build vacuum-tube circuits, telephone lines, and long-distance power transmission lines.

The device MIT built was actually similar to the electrical meters found on most homes, which measure the amount of wattage used. The machine was very good at solving mathematical equations, and, in 1930, Bush improved it so it could solve even more complex equations. He named this modified version the differential analyzer. It was the first analog computer.

In 1932, a major discovery changed the world forever. At Cavendish Laboratory in Cambridge, England, John Cockcroft and Ernest Walton split the atom for the first time. The neutron had been discovered only a few weeks earlier, and later that year, an American named Carl Anderson discovered the positron.

Ultimately, splitting the atom, along with the discovery of nuclear fission in 1939, would lead to the ability to construct an atomic bomb. This would give the world more destructive power than it had ever had before. On a more positive note, it also enabled the production of energy by nuclear power.

In nuclear energy, energy is released by the process of nuclear fission, when the nucleus of one atom is split by the impact of another atom. Nuclear fusion, which also produces energy, happens when the nuclei of two atoms collide and form one single nucleus, also releasing energy. Atomic bombs use either fission or fusion to create tremendous energy when they detonate.

In 2006, the International Astronomical Union announced that Pluto would no longer be considered a planet because of new rules about what actually constituted a planet. Since then, Pluto has been classified as a dwarf planet.

DIFFERENTIAL ANALYZER

Learn more about the differential analyzer at this site. How is it different from today's computers?

differential analyzer MIT

PS

BUILDING IN TOUGH TIMES

Many famous buildings and other structures were built during the 1930s in the Art Deco style. Art Deco was used extensively for public places, such as railroad stations and movie theaters, as well as ocean liners, amusement parks, and in public works projects.

Developed in Europe in the 1920s, Art Deco was very popular in the United States by the 1930s. It was characterized by clean, simple, "streamlined" shapes, symmetrical stylized or geometric shapes, and a combination of natural and manmade materials. The Chrysler Building in New York City is a prime example of Art Deco style.

The Empire State Building, which was planned during the 1920s, was actually constructed during the first years of the Depression. The Coca-Cola Building in Los Angeles, California, was built in the Moderne style. This style of Art Deco architecture featured long lines, curved shapes, and nautical touches.

[Built in 1939, the Coca-Cola Building looks like a large ship with portholes.]

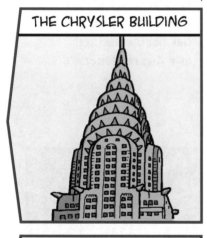

THE CHRYSLER BUILDING

THE COCA-COLA BUILDING

THE GOLDEN GATE BRIDGE

Construction of the Golden Gate Bridge in San Francisco started in 1933. It is still called one of the greatest engineering accomplishments of all time. Spanning more than a mile, it crosses the channel between San Francisco Bay and the Pacific Ocean. The Golden Gate Bridge is one of the most recognizable structures in the United States.

Other famous structures of the 1930s include the Hoover Dam, which dammed the Colorado River and created Lake Mead. Today, Hoover Dam is a popular tourist attraction that draws millions of visitors each year.

The 1930s saw the creation of the WPA "rustic" style of buildings, built in many of the country's national parks as lodges and other structures. These buildings incorporated native materials as well as construction materials and styles that were native to the area where they were built.

INVENTING THE FUTURE

Do you ever think about the next advances in science and technology? People did back then, too. Igor Sikorsky, a Russian engineer and inventor who moved to the United States, invented the first four-engine airplane in 1913. He then spent decades designing and building the first working helicopter, which he finished and test flew in 1939. Sikorsky helicopters are sold all over the world today.

The turbojet engine was also invented during the 1930s by two different men working separately without knowing what the other was doing. Dr. Hans von Ohain is given credit for designing the first operational jet engine, but Frank Whittle was the first to actually get a patent for a jet engine. However, von Ohain's jet engine was the first to successfully fly in 1939.

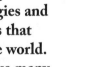

Many new inventions of the 1930s paved the way for technologies and conveniences that improved the world. Today, we take many of these for granted, such as the electron microscope, radar, the first synthetic rubber (neoprene), nylon stockings, and Teflon nonstick coating for pans.

IMAGINE LIFE WITHOUT . . .

Some of the things invented during the 1930s are things that it's hard to imagine living without, including chocolate chip cookies, frozen food, and ballpoint pens!

Ruth Wakefield and her husband, Kenneth, ran the Toll House Inn in Whitman, Massachusetts, in the 1930s. Ruth was in charge of the baking, and according to legend, she was baking chocolate cookies one day when she realized that she had run out of the kind of chocolate needed. Instead, she decided to chop up a bar of baking chocolate and put that in the dough, hoping it would melt and create chocolate cookies. Instead, the chocolate chunks remained intact, and Toll House chocolate chip cookies were born!

Clarence Birdseye is the man to thank for inventing a method to quick-freeze food. This allows us to have frozen pizzas and chicken nuggets available with just the push of a few buttons on the microwave. It also gives us fruits and veggies available all year long, even in winter.

> Birdseye invented a system of packing fresh food into waxed cardboard boxes and flash-freezing them under high pressure.

General Foods bought Birdseye's patents and trademarks in 1929 for an amazing sum of $22 million! The first frozen foods marketed to the public, including vegetables, fruits, seafood, and frozen meat, were sold in 1930 in Springfield, Massachusetts, under the name Bird's Eye Frosted Foods.

In 1938, Nestlé invented the first freeze-dried instant coffee. Freeze-drying was a process that removed water using a vacuum process while freezing the substance. It was used extensively during World War II to preserve blood plasma and penicillin.

The country of Brazil, which was suffering from a surplus of coffee, had asked for Nestlé's help. The company found a way to freeze-dry brewed coffee into a powder form that could be reconstituted with hot water. Nestlé's instant coffee, called Nescafé, was first marketed in Switzerland, but it became very popular in the United States.

> There were many new inventions that made office tasks easier, such as Scotch tape, ballpoint pens, and photocopiers.

Richard Drew, an engineer who worked for the 3M Corporation (3M stands for Minnesota Mining and Manufacturing), invented clear adhesive tape for the baking and food packaging industries. He later realized that people were using it to mend torn paper and book pages. This ability to mend torn items was especially important during the Great Depression, when every penny counted.

The brand name "Scotch tape" supposedly came from a painter who was trying a sample of the 3M tape that wasn't working well. He said in frustration, "Take this tape back to those Scotch bosses of yours and tell them to put more adhesive on it!"

The ballpoint pen was another invention from the Great Depression. A journalist from Hungary named Laszlo Biro noticed that the ink used on newspapers dried quickly and didn't smudge, unlike the ink that people used when they wrote with fountain pens.

FREEZE IT

Birdseye was not the first person to find ways to preserve food through freezing on a commercial level. As early as 1915, in Labrador, Canada, fish was being frozen in salt and ice and then sold. In 1921, Paul Peterson built an "indirect freezer," which froze food by packing it into containers and submerging it in liquid refrigerant. In 1923, Gordon F. Taylor began freezing whole fish by moving them on a conveyer belt where they were sprayed with cold water and then frozen with brine. By the time Birdseye began experimenting with his own freezing process, frozen food had been around for 50 years. He just found a better way to freeze it.

1930s FACTOID

Carlson's copier weighed almost 650 pounds, was the size of two washing machines, and was prone to suddenly catching on fire. But it would eventually change offices forever.

The ink required a different kind of nib, or point, because it was thicker than regular pen ink. So Biro invented a new kind of pen tip that had a tiny ball bearing. The bearing picked up ink from a cartridge and transferred it to the paper. In 1938, he invented the first ballpoint pen.

On October 22, 1938, in a small apartment in Queens, New York, another invention was born that no office can imagine being without today: the photocopier. Chester Carlson used static electricity created by a handkerchief, dry powder, and light to make the first photocopy, which consisted of the words "10-22-38 Astoria." It would be another 20 years before the technology would be marketed, when the Xerox Company started selling its first copier.

> The world's very first parking meter, called the Park-O-Meter No. 1, was installed in Oklahoma City, Oklahoma, on July 16, 1935.

Carl C. Magee invented the meter as a way for the city to cope with the increasing number of cars trying to park downtown. Having to pay for parking made people less likely to leave their cars in one spot for very long, and some people stopped parking entirely. This solved some of the parking congestion while creating revenue for the city. Within five years, there were 140,000 parking meters operating throughout the United States.

ENTERTAINING INVENTIONS

Some of the most important inventions made it possible for people to enjoy their favorite leisure activities in new ways. In 1931, for the first time, full-color movies with sound became common, thanks to Technicolor. FM radio and records that played in stereo sound also became popular.

The technologies that would make television possible were also developing during the 1930s, building on previous inventions. In 1930, the British Broadcasting Corporation (BBC) was already broadcasting regularly on television, and the first commercial had aired.

By 1933, Iowa State University was broadcasting twice a week. In 1937, the Central Broadcasting Service (CBS) radio network began developing television. Television was demonstrated to the public at the 1939 world's fair in New York City and the Golden Gate International Exposition in San Francisco. For many people, this was their first exposure to television.

TV CARTOONS

There were many cartoons introduced to television in the 1930s, including *Mickey Mouse* and *Felix the Cat*. What do you notice about the sound?

1930s TV cartooons

For people who traveled on airplanes, the 1930s also saw the introduction of stewards and stewardesses, who are now called "flight attendants." In the early 1930s, male stewards served on airplane flights, helping passengers get on board, assisting with their baggage, and making sure they did not smoke.

By the late 1930s, the first female stewardesses were hired by United Airlines. They were registered nurses, because the airlines thought they would be able to assist passengers who became ill during the flight, as well as make passengers feel comfortable and safe. The first stewardesses made only $1 an hour and worked an average of 100 hours a month.

[
When World War II broke out, most nurses joined the military, so the airlines started hiring stewardesses who were not nurses.
]

Inventions and innovations in science and everyday life helped move the United States toward the modern world, even in the midst of the Great Depression. But as the country moved through the decade, other events were brewing around the world that would change everything, for both better and worse.

KEY QUESTIONS

- Why were there so many new inventions in the 1930s, even as the population struggled economically?

- What inventions from the 1930s do you use today?

HELP WANTED

In the 1930s, attendants on airline flights were called stewardesses, and they were a new addition to air flight. As stewardesses became more common in air travel, airlines put into place many restrictions and guidelines governing how they dressed, how they looked, and even how much they weighed!

- **Research the history of flight attendants.** What was the job like and who were the women who worked as stewardesses? Was it a well-paying job? Was it glamorous or prestigious?

- **Create an illustrated timeline of how the job developed and changed from the 1930s to today.** Include photographs that show the changes in uniforms and hairstyles. How have the requirements for appearance, education, and gender evolved over certain eras? Also include vintage help wanted advertisements for stewardesses. What else can you find that shows how this profession has changed?

> To investigate more, create a graph showing how many men and women were employed as flight attendants between 1930 and today. Also include on the graph the average pay for attendants during this time span. Does the pay rate seem to change depending on how many men or women were employed at a certain time? Compare the guidelines for dress and appearance that were imposed on stewards and stewardesses for each decade.

VOCAB LAB

Write down what you think each word means: **Art Deco**, **innovation**, **symmetrical**, **radar**, and **public works**.

Compare your definitions with those of your friends or classmates. Did you all come up with the same meanings? Turn to the text and glossary if you need help.

FREEZE-DRIED!

Freeze-dried coffee made its debut during the 1930s. It was a new way to preserve food. Not only did the process of freeze-drying keep food from spoiling, but it was also easier to cook later on. You can try your own version of freeze-drying using apples, potatoes, or carrots.

• **With a knife, slice your food items as thinly as you can.** The thinner the slices, the faster they freeze.

• **Place the slices on a tray or plate that fits into your freezer and slide the tray into the freezer.** Do this as soon as possible after you cut them, before the slices can discolor.

• **Check the slices in a half hour.** They should already be solidly frozen by then. Leave the slices in the freezer for at least a week, and check them to see if they are dry. As they freeze, the water in the slices is sublimating, which means the water is changing from solid water to water vapor.

• **After a week, remove one slice from the freezer and let it thaw.** If it turns black, it was not yet dry. Let the other slices continue to freeze and dry. When you remove a slice and it does not turn black, then all the water has been removed.

• **Once they are thoroughly dried, you can eat the slices.** Try reconstituting them in boiling water, or you can just eat them the way they are. What do they taste like?

To investigate more, try freeze-drying lots of different kinds of foods. Which foods work best? Why?

Chapter 7

War and Recovery

What ended the Great Depression?

The entry of the United States into World War II was an important factor in bringing the country out of its decade-long economic depression.

What finally ended the Great Depression? The standard answer is the advent of World War II. A country fighting a war needs weapons, trucks, and ammunition. It needs uniforms, food, and tents. Even before the United States entered the war at the end of 1941, the country was producing many of these things for Great Britain and France, which were at war with Germany by 1939. There was a sudden need for people to fill production jobs and many men, and some women, joined the military. All of a sudden there were plenty of jobs and unemployment fell. Gradually, the economy improved.

Modern economists argue that this is too simple a view, and that economics don't improve just because of war. It would take more economic incentives to make sure that the U.S. economy didn't slip back into a depression following World War II. But certainly the war did jump-start the economy and help it back onto its feet.

WAR CLOUDS

The economy didn't stay the same throughout the 1930s. After 1933, when many of Roosevelt's New Deal programs were in place, it seemed as if things were steadily improving. But then, in 1937, another sharp recession hit.

The 1937 recession was due in part to the Federal Reserve deciding to increase the amount of money it had in reserve. What did this mean? There was less money available for public programs, including the relief program. The economy slowly began improving again the next year, but the 1937 recession reversed many of the economic gains that the United States had struggled to make since 1929. It prolonged the Great Depression until the end of the decade.

[
Even more disturbing than the fluctuating economy were the signs coming from events overseas.
]

Many other countries had also been suffering from economic depressions, and this allowed for the rise of several extreme political movements. People who were distressed from having no money and no jobs were more vulnerable to the ideas of extreme leaders. The first of these leaders came into power in the early 1930s, at the same time that Roosevelt was being elected.

Adolf Hitler, the chancellor of Germany, was given absolute government power by the German congress, called the Reichstag. This meant that Germany was now a Nazi dictatorship, not a democracy.

"THE WAR OF THE WORLDS"

On October 30, 1938, Orson Welles of the Mercury Theater put on a radio dramatization of H.G. Wells' book, *The War of the Worlds*, in which aliens invade the earth. The broadcast was framed as a "breaking news" story and was so realistic that many listeners thought it was real and panicked. Even though the program had been scheduled and the announcer initially introduced it as a story, not real news, people all over the country called radios, newspapers, and police to find out what was going on and what they should do. This national hysteria showed that Americans, having heard about Hitler's invasions in Europe, feared that the same thing could easily happen to them, whether from Nazis or aliens.

[Germany was still reeling from its defeat in World War I.]

The Treaty of Versailles, which ended World War I, imposed many harsh terms on the Germans. They had to repay some of the costs of the war, called reparations, which caused great hardship for most Germans. Germany was not allowed to have a large army, navy, or air force. German citizens were angry about the terms of the Versailles peace treaty and many were struggling to have enough to eat and to keep a roof over their heads.

Hitler seemed like the kind of strong leader who would bring back a stable economy and also stand up to the rest of the world. Hitler and his Nazi political party emphasized nationalism—the love of country that was more important than doing the right thing. For a population that was angry about the way it was treated after World War I, Hitler's leadership and nationalism made them feel more secure and better about themselves.

According to historians Walter Rinderle and Bernard Norling:

> Nazism seemed to many just an extreme version of what [most Germans] had always believed in or taken for granted. It was nationalistic, respectful of the armed forces, socially conservative, disdainful of laziness, hostile to eccentric or incomprehensive ideas that came from cities, disapproving of homosexuals and other unconventional human types, and avid to achieve 'greatness' for Germany. They welcomed parts of the Nazi political and social smorgasbord and told themselves that the rest was less important or was not meant seriously.

Hitler was able to convince the German people that he could make things better for them. He created an ideal blond-haired, blue-eyed German, called an Aryan. Then Hitler began exterminating Jewish people and any other groups of people who weren't part of that German ideal.

The Holocaust was one of the most devastating aspects of World War II. As part of Hitler's purge of those who were not the pure-blooded Aryans that he considered to be superior, 6 million Jews were persecuted and killed. This represented 78 percent of the Jews who lived in Europe at that time. Approximately 5 million Gypsies, other minorities, homosexuals, and handicapped people were also killed in the camps.

[
Execution camps were specially constructed as killing facilities, where large numbers of people were systematically murdered in gas chambers.
]

Hitler justified the terrible things he did as part of the mission of the German people.

HITLER'S ARYAN RACE

Hitler believed that only one type of person was an acceptable example of the human race. He said, "What we must fight for is to safeguard the existence and reproduction of our race and our people, the sustenance of our children and the purity of our blood, the freedom and independence of the fatherland, so that our people may mature for the fulfillment of the mission allotted it by the creator of the universe."

DECLARATIONS OF WAR

When the Twin Towers were attacked in September 2001, many people compared it to the attack on Pearl Harbor 60 years before. Both presidents at the time, Franklin Roosevelt in 1941 and George W. Bush in 2001, made speeches declaring war on the people who initiated the attack. Listen to both speeches. Are there similarities between the two? How did each president use his speech to motivate the American people?

🔍 Roosevelt Pearl Harbor address

🔍 Bush war terror speech

Hitler's campaign of murder continued until the end of WWII, in 1945. Many American servicemen helped to liberate prisoners from concentration camps. This devastating experience first brought the news of these camps' existence to the rest of the world. Colonel William W. Quinn, who served with the U.S. 7th Army, described the scene at the Dachau concentration camp: "There our troops found sights, sounds, and stenches horrible beyond belief, cruelties so enormous as to be incomprehensible to the normal mind."

A TERRIBLE TIMELINE

Hitler was not the only extreme military dictator coming into power during the 1930s. Japan saw General Hideki Tojo come to power, while Italy was home to dictator Benito Mussolini. Ultimately, these three rulers and their countries would form the Axis powers of World War II. As the 1930s unfolded, these powers became stronger and stronger.

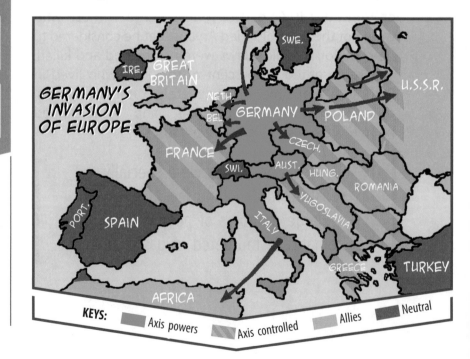

In 1936, a treaty was signed between Hitler's Nazi Germany and the fascist Italian government under Mussolini. This was followed by a pact between the Nazis and Japan against Russia, where communism was developing under dictator Joseph Stalin. In 1937, Japan invaded China. And then Hitler started his march into the rest of Europe, annexing Austria in 1938 and invading Poland in 1939. War finally broke out in Europe that year, with France and England declaring war on Germany. Countries fighting against the Axis powers were called the Allies.

While President Roosevelt supported France and England, he officially kept a position of neutrality. Americans wanted nothing to do with another European war barely 20 years after the end of World War I. However, during this time the United States quietly built up its military.

America's isolationism ended on December 7, 1941, when the Japanese bombed the U.S. Naval Base at Pearl Harbor, Hawaii. President Roosevelt gave a speech on the radio the next day.

> Yesterday, December 7th, 1941—a date which will live in infamy—the United States of America was suddenly and deliberately attacked by naval and air forces of the Empire of Japan. Hostilities exist. There is no blinking at the fact that our people, our territory and our interests are in grave danger. With confidence in our armed forces, with the unbounding determination of our people, we will gain the inevitable triumph. So help us God. I ask that the Congress declare that since the unprovoked and dastardly attack by Japan on Sunday, December 7th, 1941, a state of war has existed between the United States and the Japanese Empire.

Attach on Pearl Harbor, 1941

photo credit: U.S. National Archives

PEARL HARBOR

More than 2,400 people were killed during the attack on Pearl Harbor. Several Navy ships were heavily damaged or completely lost. This video shows some of the original footage of the attack on Pearl Harbor.

Pear Harbor color film

As a result of the attack, the United States officially entered World War II when Roosevelt signed the declaration of war on December 8, 1941, at 4 p.m. Three days later, Japan's allies, Italy and Germany, both declared war on the United States, and Congress immediately responded by declaring war on them. War had begun.

OUT OF THE DEPRESSION . . . AND INTO THE WAR

How did something as terrible as a war help fix something as terrible as the Great Depression? Jobs. As the first rumors of war in Europe and Asia surfaced, U.S. defense manufacturing quietly increased. Once war was officially declared, factories quickly went back into full production in order to make all the equipment, weapons, and hardware necessary for fighting a war in the 1940s.

> Factories began making airplanes, tanks, vehicles, weapons, uniforms, and anything else that was needed for the fighting and survival of American soldiers.

All of this production required people to work in the factories. By 1942, record numbers of people had jobs and unemployment had nearly disappeared. This was coupled with the beginning of the draft, which meant that all able-bodied young men were conscripted into the armed forces, leaving fewer people to fill the factory positions.

Women found an unexpected benefit of the war and the sudden shortage of workers for factories and offices. All of a sudden, they were a vital addition to the workforce.

Many women had felt relegated to households and childcare, especially during the long years of the Great Depression, when even men could not find jobs. The sudden opportunities that the war brought were exciting.

By 1945, 2.2 million women were working in factories as well as in the war industries.

> Above all, the pay was much better in the factories than the pay for traditional women's jobs, such working as a nanny or a teacher.

The Great Depression ended, but at the tremendous cost of world war. And even as the hard times of the 1930s began to fade, they left a legacy that would not be forgotten for a generation.

A LEGACY OF HARD TIMES

For those people who lived through the Great Depression, either as adults or as children, the 1930s left a legacy in their lives that never really went away. Many of these people had a strong work ethic—they felt that jobs were important and working was a priority. They were financially conservative and distrustful of investments. They were even distrustful of banks, despite the New Deal measures that created insurance for deposits in banks.

Many would always be frugal, refusing to throw away things that could be mended. They might be cautious about new purchases and the use of credit. Some would never possess a credit card, buy a car with a payment plan, or take out a mortgage to buy a home.

Of course, the effects of the Great Depression depended on the experiences of the people who lived through it. Some people lived through extreme hardship, while others only felt minor inconveniences and continued to live fairly comfortable and secure lives.

NEW ROLES FOR WOMEN

Women's roles in the workforce began to change. According to the National Women's History Museum:

"Wages in munitions plants and aircraft factories averaged more than those for traditional female jobs. Women abandoned traditional jobs, particularly domestic service, to work in war production plants offering 40 percent higher wages. Many women were recruited to migrate from rural areas to take on the dangerous but necessary work."

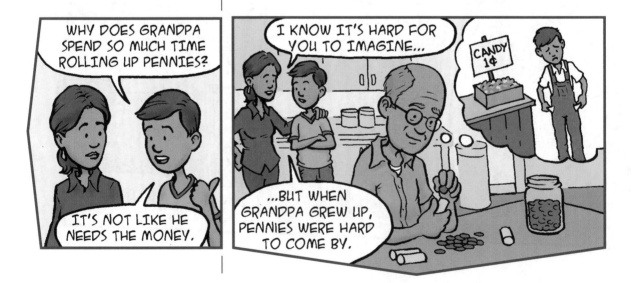

> But almost everyone who experienced the 1930s firsthand had some residual attitude that colored how they lived the rest of their lives and the lessons they taught their children and grandchildren.

Those who were born later never experienced this type of widespread economic crisis. But in cycles that repeat themselves, people continue to overextend themselves by misusing credit. Some banks have continued to do business in ways that hurt many people.

The 2008 recession that resulted in high unemployment rates was caused by a crisis in the mortgage industry. Many people had been given mortgages by banks for homes that they could not really afford, then these risky mortgages were sold and resold. When housing values fell, it started a chain reaction of bank failures and corporate bankruptcies.

The 1930s are remembered for the Great Depression, but it was also a time of new inventions, new products, and big steps toward the modern lives we live today. Despite the hardships, they were still years of family and friendship and community, perhaps more so because times were so hard and it drew people together. And that is one of the best legacies of such a turbulent time.

The 2008 Great Recession was the worst recession since the Great Depression. The stock market crashed, millions of people lost their jobs, and many lost their homes to foreclosure because they could not pay their mortgages.

KEY QUESTIONS

- Why were many of the people who lived through the Great Depression frugal and thrifty?
- What role does credit play in your life? Are you a frugal spender?
- Do you think the Great Depression could happen in your lifetime?

ROSIE THE RIVETER

Women became vital members of the work force during World War II, and their efforts in factories and other war industries were important to the success of Allied troops. One of the most familiar posters of the time showed Rosie the Riveter rolling up her sleeve and saying, "We Can Do It!" Since WWII, the Rosie image has been used and modified for many types of advertising campaigns involving women.

VOCAB LAB

Write down what you think each word means: **frugal, treaty, concentration camp, isolationism, nationalism,** and **dictator.**

Compare your definitions with those of your friends or classmates. Did you all come up with the same meanings? Turn to the text and glossary if you need help.

MORE 1930S SLANG

Tin can, flivver: a car

"You shred it, wheat": you said it

- **Research the Rosie poster image and see how many different variations you can find.** Print out copies and create a display of the different images. Which ones seem to be effective and which aren't? What kind of message is the image best suited to?

- **Create your own version of the Rosie the Riveter poster.** You can either draw by hand or create a digital image. How can you use the image to send a message about a current issue?

To investigate more, consider the kinds of images used today to present current opinions or seek action. Find examples of posters, web pages, or other media that convey strong messages by using an image that is both intriguing and easy to relate to. Can you think of a modern advertising or public service campaign slogan or image that has had a lasting impact?

MAPPING THE WAR

The Nazis and other Axis powers were already moving across Europe before the United States entered the war in 1941. World War II was also fought in Asia and across the Pacific Ocean.

- **Research the events of the war in Europe.** Start with the first Nazi invasions of other countries, and create a map that shows the movement of the Nazi and Axis forces across Europe, both during the 1930s and as the United States came into the war. You can find interactive maps of the war here.

 National Archives WWII map

- **Now research the events of the war in the Pacific.** Start with the Japanese invasion of China in 1937. Create a map that shows the movement of the Japanese across Asia and the Pacific Ocean.

map Japanese advance Pacific interactive

To investigate more, find animated films that served as propaganda during the war. The Walt Disney animation studio made many cartoons about the war, some of which were serious in nature, some comical. All of them were intended to share information about the war or the enemy. Research these films and download one to share with your classmates. How does creating films in an animation format affect how the message is told. How does it influence how the message is received by the audience?

PEARL HARBOR

The Japanese attack on Pearl Harbor, Hawaii, on December 7, 1941, brought the United States into World War II. It was a huge shock to the nation.

- **Find an audio recording of a breaking news report about the attack on Pearl Harbor, describing the event as it took place or shortly after.** Also, find newspaper reports of the attack. Some ideas for keyword searches are Pearl Harbor, news, primary source.

- **Write a script with your own version of the breaking news.** You can assign parts to your classmates to act out. Describe the attack as it happens, with details about what is taking place, the destruction, and the reactions of both Navy personnel and civilians. Use sound effects to make your news report realistic.

- **Find an audio version or a transcript of President Roosevelt's speech following Pearl Harbor and announcing the declaration of war.** Read it aloud to the class following your radio play of the attack. How might you rewrite this speech for today's audience?

HANG IN THERE!

Inspirational posters of the 1930s and WWII generally fell into three categories: advocating for government relief programs during the Depression, things the average American could do every day for the war effort, and the evils of the Axis powers and how they might gain information about America by spying on regular citizens who weren't careful about what they said. The National Archives has a large collection of posters from this era.

PS

National Archives poster art WWII

Library Congress WPA posters

> To investigate more, research breaking news reports following the destruction of the Twin Towers on September 11, 2001. Compare a variety of sources (online, audio, video, and written) to audio and written reports of Pearl Harbor. How are they similar? How are they different?

accentuate: to emphasize something or make it more pronounced.

aerodynamic: having a shape that reduces the amount of drag created by air passing around or over it.

affluence: the state of having a great deal of money or wealth.

Allies: the nations that fought against the Axis powers during WWII.

annex: to incorporate territory into a country.

aristocratic: having to do with people of high rank or privilege or the elite.

Art Deco: a decorative art style of the 1920s and 1930s, which used geometric shapes and strong colors.

Aryan: a member or descendant of the prehistoric people who settled Europe.

assembly line: a series of workers and machines that assemble products in a factory.

atom: the basic unit of a chemical element.

atomic bomb: a bomb that is powered by the nuclear energy released by splitting an atom.

Axis powers: the countries of Germany, Italy, and Japan, which fought against the Allies in WWII.

bailout: giving financial assistance to a failing business to save it from collapse.

bootlegger: someone who illegally transports alcoholic beverages.

bread line: a group of people lined up to receive free food.

capitalist: having to do with capitalism, where the economy is controlled by manufacturing and production in the hands of the wealthy, rather than by government or collective wealth.

characteristic: a feature or quality that belongs to a person, place, or thing and helps identify it.

civil rights: the rights of citizens to have political and social equality and freedom.

commerce: buying and selling, especially on a large scale.

communism: a political theory where all property is publicly owned and each person works according to their ability and needs.

concentration camp: during WWII, large camps where Jews and other minorities were imprisoned by the Nazis and forced to perform hard labor or exterminated.

congestion: when something is filled to excess, crowded, or overburdened.

conscripted: drafted or called up for military service.

conservative: holding to traditional attitudes and values and reluctant to change, especially about politics or religion.

consumer: a person who buys goods and services.

contemporary: existing at the same time.

corset: a woman's tight fitting undergarment, meant to shape their figures.

credit: paying for something later or over time.

crops: cultivated plants, especially grains, fruits, and vegetables.

currency: money, such as bills or coins, used as a method of exchange.

debt: money owed to another person, a business, or an institution.

dictator: a ruler with total power over a country, usually achieved through force.

discrimination: treating people unfairly or with prejudice, usually based on their race, age, or sex.

dividend: a sum of money paid regularly by a company to its shareholders.

GLOSSARY

drought: a long period of dry weather, especially one that damages crops.

Dust Bowl: the region of the south central United States that was damaged in the 1920s and 1930s by persistent dust storms that killed off crops and livestock.

dust storm: a strong wind that carries clouds of dust, dirt, and sand across a large area.

economic depression: a lasting, long-term downturn in a country's economic activity.

economic: having to do with the resources and wealth of a country.

economizing: avoiding waste or extravagance, being frugal.

economy: a system of producing and consuming goods and services.

electron microscope: a type of microscope that uses a beam of electrons to create an image of the specimen.

endurance: the ability or strength to continue or last despite fatigue, stress, or obstacles.

exploit: to take advantage of.

exterminate: to destroy completely or get rid of.

fad: an intense enthusiasm for something that is shared by many people but doesn't usually last.

fascist: a follower of a dictator who holds absolute power over a country.

Federal Reserve: the central bank of the United States.

fluctuating: changing continually, shifting back and forth.

forage: to search for food or other provisions, often from the natural world.

foreclosure: when a homeowner is unable to make payments on property, resulting in the bank taking possession of the property and evicting the owners.

freeze dry: to preserve something by rapidly freezing it and then removing the ice using a vacuum process.

frugal: simple, plain, sparing, especially when it comes to food or saving money.

gangster: a member of a gang of violent criminals.

generation: all of the people who were born and are living at about the same time.

goods: commodities, goods, materials, and other products that are manufactured or created.

gravity: the force that attracts a body toward the center of the earth.

Great Depression: a time in United States history when the economy struggled and many people lost their money, homes, and jobs.

hoarding: to accumulate something for future use, often hiding it in a secret place.

Holocaust: the killing of millions of Jews and others by the Nazis during WWII.

hydraulic: operated or moved by using the motion of water or other liquids.

inaugural: having to do with a presidential inauguration; marking the beginning of something new.

individualism: a social theory that favors the individual's freedom of action over the control of the state or government.

inflation: a rise in prices combined with a decline in the purchasing power of money.

innovation: a new method, idea, or product.

insured: to be covered or protected by insurance.

investment: a purchase made by a person in hopes of a larger future return.

investor: a person who agrees to give time or money to an enterprise.

isolationism: a policy of remaining apart from and uninvolved with the politics of other countries.

liberal: open to new behavior and opinions and willing to discard traditional values.

lucrative: making a great deal of money or profit.

manufacturing: to make large quantities of products, usually in factories.

margin: to deposit an amount of money with a broker as security for a transaction or account.

middle class: the social group that includes professional and business people and their families.

migrant: a person who moves from place to place to find work.

minority: a part of the population that is different, or is a smaller group.

mobster: a gangster or member of a group of violent criminals.

mortgage: a legal agreement where a person borrows money to buy property and pays it back during a number of years.

munitions: materials used in war, especially weapons and ammunition.

nationalism: devotion or loyalty to one's country, patriotism.

natural disaster: a natural event, such as a fire or flood, that causes great damage.

Nazi: a member of the National Socialist German Workers' Party during WWII.

neutrality: the policy of a country not to participate in wars between other countries.

neutron: the part of an atom that has no positive or negative charge.

New Deal: a set of programs and policies introduced by President Roosevelt to promote economic recovery and social reform during the Great Depression.

nomination: the act of proposing or recommending someone for an office or position.

nonintervention: a policy where a government does not interfere in the affairs of other nations.

nuclear fission: a nuclear reaction where a heavy nucleus splits when impacted by another particle.

nuclear power: power that is generated in a nuclear reactor using the fission process.

optimism: hope and confidence about the future or how something will work out.

orbit: the curved path of a planetary body or a spacecraft around another planet, star, or moon.

overextend: to financially obligate oneself beyond a manageable limit.

patent: a government license that gives an inventor or creator sole right to make and sell a product or invention.

perishable: food that is likely to decay or go bad quickly.

persecute: to abuse or ill-treat someone based on their race or their political or religious beliefs.

plight: a dangerous, difficult, or unfortunate situation.

positron: an atomic particle with the same mass as an electron, but with a positive charge instead of a negative one.

prairie: a large, open area of grassland.

primary source: a document or physical object that was created during the time that a scholar is studying.

progressive: in favor of progress, change, improvement, or reform.

Prohibition: a law that forbid manufacturing and selling alcohol in the United States between 1920 and 1933.

pronouncement: a formal or authoritative statement.

GLOSSARY

propaganda: misleading or biased information meant to change public opinion or publicize a particular cause.

prosperity: being in a successful; flourishing, or thriving condition.

prosperous: financially successful; bringing wealth or success.

public works: roads, schools reservoirs, and other building projects carried out by a government for the community.

publicity: notice or attention given to someone or something by the media.

purge: to get rid of, move, or eliminate something.

quintuplet: one of five children born at the same time from the same mother.

radar: a system for detecting aircraft, ships, and other objects using high-frequency electromagnetic waves.

recession: a temporary economic slowdown.

reconstitute: to return a dehydrated food to a liquid state by adding water.

reparations: compensation for war damage that is paid by the losing power.

respiratory: having to do with breathing.

revenue: income, especially for a company or organization.

saloon: a place to sell and drink alcohol.

scavenging: searching for and collecting anything useable from trash and other discarded materials.

segregation: the enforced separation of different racial groups in a community or country.

shanty: a small, crudely built shack.

shantytown: an area, usually on the outskirts of a city or town, of small rough shacks.

social welfare: a government system that provides assistance to needy people and families.

society: the group of people living together in an organized community.

solvent: able to pay one's debts, having enough money.

speakeasy: an illegal store or nightclub selling alcohol during Prohibition.

stock market: a market where shares of companies, or stocks, are bought and sold.

symmetrical: made up of exactly similar parts facing each other; even or balanced.

tariff: taxes, duties, or charges imposed by a government on import or exports.

terrace: to shape agricultural land into raised sections with vertical or sloping sides, similar to steps.

thrifty: being very careful with money.

topsoil: the fertile, upper part or layer of soil.

transitive: changing.

treaty: a formal agreement between countries.

turbulent: characterized by conflict, disorder, or confusion; out of control.

unconstitutional: unauthorized, or inconsistent with the United States Constitution.

unemployed: not having a job.

unemployment rate: the number of people who don't have jobs in a certain area or time.

Venn diagram: a diagram that uses circles to represent sets and their relationships.

wealth: having a great deal of valuable property or money.

welfare: financial support given to needy people.

zeppelin: a large German dirigible or airship, similar to a blimp.

⊙ BOOKS

Building History: The Hoover Dam. Lusted, Marcia Amidon, Lucent Books, 2003.

Children of the Dust Bowl: The True Story of the School at Weedpatch Camp.
Stanley, Jerry, Crown Publishers,1992.

Daily Life in the United States, 1920-1940: How Americans Lived Through the Roaring Twenties and the Great Depression. Kyvig, David E., Ivan R. Dee, 2004.

Fashions of a Decade: The 1930s. Costantino, Maria, Chelsea House, 2006.

Frozen in Time: Clarence Birdseye's Outrageous Idea About Frozen Food.
Kurlansky, Mark, Delacorte Press, 2014.

Restless Spirit: The Life and Works of Dorothea Lange. Partridge, Elizabeth, Penguin Books, 1998.

Riding the Rails: Teenagers on the Move During the Great Depression.
Uys, Errol Lincoln, TV Books, 1999.

Since Yesterday: The 1930s in America. Allen, Frederick Lewis, Harper & Row, 1986.

The Great Depression in United States History. Fremon, David K., Enslow Publishers, 2014.

The Great Depression: The Jazz Age, Prohibition, and the Great Depression, 1921-1937.
Bingham, Jane, Chelsea House, 2011.

Understanding American History: The Great Depression.
George, Linda and Charles, Referencepoint Press, 2012.

Years of Dust: The Story of the Dust Bowl. Marrin, Albert, Dutton Children's Books, 2009.

⊙ PLACES TO VISIT

Franklin D. Roosevelt Presidential Library and Museum: www.fdrlibrary.marist.edu

Herbert Hoover Presidential Library and Museum: www.hoover.archives.gov

Hoover Dam: www.usbr.gov/lc/hooverdam

Empire State Building: www.esbnyc.com

Route 66 Museum: www.route66.org

Smithsonian National Museum of American History: americanhistory.si.edu/treasures/depression-wwii

RESOURCES

⊙ WEBSITES

The History Channel: The Great Depression: www.history.com/topics/great-depression

American Experience: Surviving the Dust Bowl: www.pbs.org/wgbh/americanexperience/films/dustbowl

The People History: 1930s News, Events, Popular Culture and Prices:
www.thepeoplehistory.com/1930s.html

Iowa Pathways: The Great Depression: www.iptv.org/iowapathways/mypath.cfm?ounid=ob_000064

America in the 1930s: xroads.virginia.edu/~1930s/front.html

American Experience: The 1930s: www.pbs.org/wgbh/americanexperience/collections/1930s

Library of Congress: Great Depression and WWII:
www.loc.gov/teachers/classroommaterials/presentationsandactivities/presentations/timeline/depwwii/newdeal

Roosevelt Institute: The New Deal: rooseveltinstitute.org/policy-and-ideasroosevelt-historyfdr/new-deal

Fashion Era: 1930s Fashion History: www.fashion-era.com/1930s

History Channel: Stock Market Crash of 1929: www.history.com/topics/1929-stock-market-crash

Federal Reserve: Stock Market Crash of 1929: www.federalreservehistory.org/Events/DetailView/74

New York Times: The Great Depression:
nytimes.com/top/reference/timestopics/subjects/g/great_depression_1930s/index.html

American Experience: Riding the Rails: www.pbs.org/wgbh/americanexperience/films/rails

⊙ QR CODE GLOSSARY

Page 4: www.nytimes.com/library/financial/index-1929-crash.html

Page 12: www.youtube.com/watch?v=iL0Qt7IF8Q4

Page 16: www.forbes.com/sites/quora/2011/11/08/how-does-the-current-economic-recession-compare-to-the-great-depression

Page 25: www.youtube.com/watch?v=PSMDPzd11ek

Page 26: www.npr.org/2008/11/15/96654742/a-depression-era-anthem-for-our-times

Page 27: www.youtube.com/watch?v=xkmo4ygPTjc

Page 28: www.youtube.com/watch?v=lSniZl_H7mE

Page 39: www.youtube.com/watch?v=nHFTtz3uucY

Page 47: www.loc.gov/pictures

Page 48: teachengineering.org/view_activity.php?url=collection/cub_/activities/cub_dams/cub_dams_lesson02_activity1.xml

Page 50: newdeal.feri.org/eleanor/er3a.htm

Page 55: www.youtube.com/watch?v=Nw4qH0jjDx8

Page 56: www.youtube.com/watch?v=dCYApJtsyd0

Page 58: www.worldpath.net/~minstrel/hobosign.htm

Page 59: http://www.nps.gov/manz/learn/photosmultimedia/dorothea-lange-gallery.htm

Page 60: www.youtube.com/watch?v=_sJZpeBw6YE

Page 65: www.nsa.gov/about/_files/cryptologic_heritage/museum/library/hobo_signs_definitions.pdf

Page 69: www.youtube.com/watch?v=TpfY8kh5lUw

Page 77: www.youtube.com/watch?v=hpbi_LQIlzE

Page 78: www.youtube.com/watch?v=tp2mrCcPPOo

Page 79: time.com/79600/the-fall-of-the-fair

Page 79: www.theatlantic.com/photo/2013/11/the-1939-new-york-worlds-fair/100620/#

Page 80: archive.org/details/SF145

Page 81: usbgf.org/learn-backgammon/rules-of-backgammon

Page 83: www.youtube.com/watch?v=YtZrXzoaJvc

Page 87: museum.mit.edu/150/22

Page 90: www.newyorker.com/culture/culture-desk/sweet-morsels-a-history-of-the-chocolate-chip-cookie

Page 93: www.youtube.com/playlist?list=PL0C16CEAA20F7764C

Page 100: www.youtube.com/watch?v=Xs0K4ApWl4g&spfreload=10

Page 102: www.youtube.com/watch?v=3VqQAf74fsE
Page 102: www.youtube.com/watch?v=_CSPbzitPL8

Page 103: www.youtube.com/watch?v=3e99lfmmDN0

Page 104: archive.org/details/RosieTheRiveter

Page 109: www.nationalarchives.gov.uk/education/worldwar2/default.htm

Page 109: www.eduplace.com/kids/socsci/books/applications/imaps/maps/g5s_u8/#top

Page 110: www.archives.gov/exhibits/powers_of_persuasion/powers_of_persuasion_intro.html
Page 110: www.loc.gov/pictures/search/?st=grid&co=wpapos

INDEX

1930s

INDEX

INDEX

National Recovery Administration, 46
natural disasters
    drought as, 4, 15, 52–55, 58, 62, 63
    Dust Bowl due to, vi, 4, 52–64
    floods as, vii, 78
    migrants/migration due to, 4, 52, 54, 56, 57, 58–61, 64
natural resources, 15–16
Nestlé, 91
New Deal, vi, vii, 31, 38–48, 89, 99
news media, 41, 75, 77–78, 80
nuclear fission and fusion, vi, 87

O

Owens, Jessie, 75–76

P

parking meters, vii, 92
Pearl Harbor attack, vii, 102, 103–104, 110
penny auctions, 24
Perkins, Frances, 40
Peterson, Paul, 91
photocopiers, vii, 92
Pluto, vi, 86, 87
prices/price controls, 14–15, 24, 53, 61, 62, 70
Prohibition, repeal of, vi, 71–72
Public Works Administration (PWA), 45
Public Works of Art Project, 89

R

radio broadcasts, vii, 41, 75, 93, 99, 100
Roaring Twenties, 2–3, 8–19, 70
Rockefeller, John D., 11
Rogers, Ginger, 74, 83
Roosevelt, Eleanor, 42–43, 50

Roosevelt, Franklin
    election of, vi, vii, 5, 31, 35
    Fireside Chats of, 41, 75
    "The Hundred Days" of, vi, 38
    inaugural speech of, 39
    New Deal under, vi, vii, 31, 38–48, 89, 99
    Pearl Harbor address and response by, 102, 103–104, 110
    race relations under, 30, 31
Rosie the Riveter, 104, 108
Route 66, 56

S

Scotch tape, 91
Seabiscuit, 76–77
Securities and Exchange Commission (SEC), 45
Securities Exchange Act (1934), vi
Sikorsky, Igor, vii, 89
Social Security Act, vii, 46
societal changes, vi, vii, 68–83
Soil Conservation Service, 61–62
sports, 70, 72, 75–77
Stalin, Joseph, 103
"The Star Spangled Banner," vi
Steinbeck, John, 26, 54, 60, 61, 74
stock market
    investing in, 9, 10, 13, 16, 18–19
    regulation of, vi, 39, 45
    Stock Market Crash of 1929, vi, 2–3, 8, 10–11, 12, 17
Superman, vii, 74

T

taxes and tariffs, 12, 14, 72
Taylor, Gordon F., 91
television, 93
Temple, Shirley, 74, 77
Tennessee Valley Authority (TVA), 46, 48
timeline, vi–vii

Tojo, Hideki, 102–103
Toll House cookies, 90
Tombaugh, Clyde W., vi, 86
trains, migration via, 25, 58–59
Truman, Harry S., 30

U

unemployment, vi, 3–5, 10, 14, 15, 16, 22–28, 107

V

veterans, Bonus Army of, vi, 26–27
von Ohain, Hans, 89

W

Wakefield, Ruth and Kenneth, 90
Walton, Ernest, vi, 87
Welles, Orson, *The War of the Worlds*, vii, 99, 100
Whittle, Frank, 89
Wilkie, Wendell, 35
women in workplace, 40, 43, 70, 94, 95, 104, 105, 106, 108
work
    government programs creating, vi, 26, 30, 31, 43–46, 47, 48, 89
    income/earnings/salaries, vii, 3, 5, 10, 23, 25, 61, 94, 105, 106
    labor regulations for, 39, 46
    migration to find, 4, 25, 26, 52, 54, 56, 57, 58–61
    minority/racial issues in, 30, 31
    unemployment, vi, 3–5, 10, 14, 15, 16, 22–28, 107
    women in workplace, 40, 43, 70, 94, 95, 104, 105, 106, 108
    World War II creating, 94, 98, 104–106, 108
Works Progress Administration (WPA), 30, 31, 44–46, 47, 89
world's fair, vi, vii, 78, 79, 93
World War I, 26
World War II, vii, 62, 91, 94, 98–110